ROCK IDOLS

A Guide to Dartmoor in 28 Tors

Illustrated, written and photographed by

Alex Murdin
Sophie Pierce

Sacred Circle, Gidleigh Common, by C F Williams, 1848

ROCK IDOLS

A Guide to Dartmoor in 28 Tors

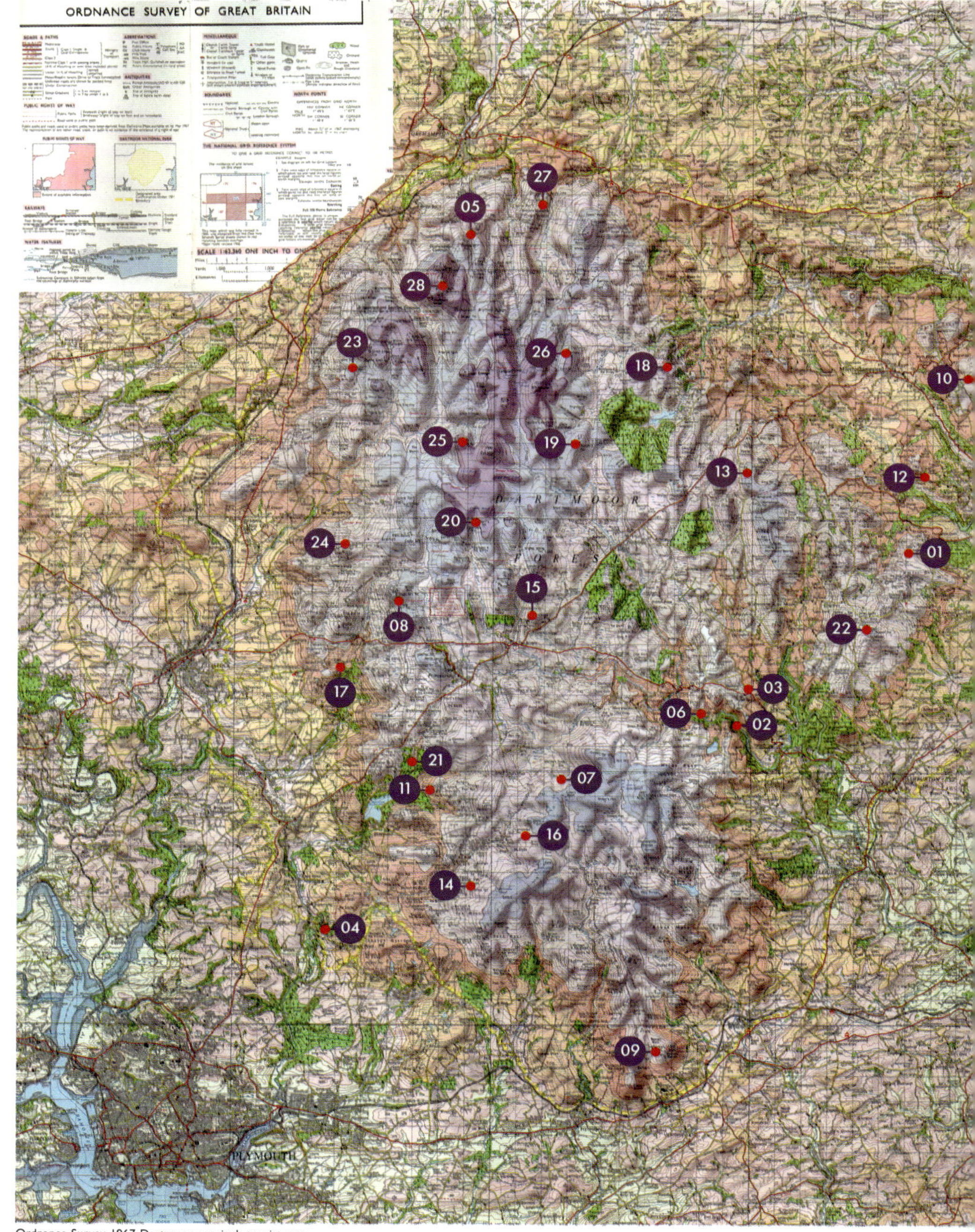

Ordnance Survey 1967 Dartmoor one-inch tourist map

CONTENTS

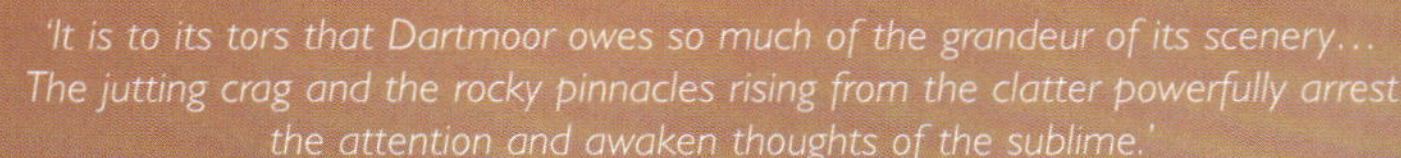

'It is to its tors that Dartmoor owes so much of the grandeur of its scenery... The jutting crag and the rocky pinnacles rising from the clatter powerfully arrest the attention and awaken thoughts of the sublime.'

William Crossing, *Gems in a Granite Setting*, 1905

'Rocks were first chosen, it seems to me, to represent the Gods from the firmness of their substance, continuing still the same, neither disappearing soon, as Fire; nor ruffled, and by drought dissipated, like Water, not wasting away like Earth; and therefore proper emblems of Strength, Shelter, Shade and Defence.'

William Borlase, *Antiquities*, 1769

'In the Druid Ages, stones of various shapes were consecrated to religion... They prostrated themselves before the rudest. In Danmonium, the Druids... professed to believe, that rocky places were the favourite abodes of their divinities. And wherever we find stones, which are at the same time massy and misshapen, there we look for the druidical gods. Vastness, in short, and rudeness were the characteristics of the Druid Rock-Idols... Thus Dartmoor would be one wide Druid temple, and its dark waste, now consecrated ground, would breathe a browner horror.'

Richard Polwhele, *Historical Views of Devonshire*, 1793

INTRODUCTION

Dim shapes looming dark and cold out of swirling mist; blue shadows melting into a river of bluebells; hazy stacks shimmering under an adder-baking summer's sun. Forbidding castles guarded by croaking ravens; granite sanctuaries set in a sea of purple heather; rocky hollows harbouring secrets. Just a few impressions of Dartmoor's tors gathered in our memory.

We moved here in the year 2000 from the flat fens of Cambridgeshire and were immediately captivated by its rugged granite landscape. At first, we explored near our home in Ashburton, becoming familiar with our local peaks: Rippon Tor, Buckland Beacon, Top Tor, Saddle Tor, and Haytor to name but a few. They became the playgrounds of our two young sons Felix and Lucian, who loved to climb them and seek out the letterboxes hidden in their crevices. As the boys grew up, we continued to explore, and over the last 25 years we have formed an increasingly strong emotional connection, as well as a fascination, with its primeval rocks.

These ancient stones radiate poetry and power. In one of the first guidebooks to Dartmoor, *A Perambulation of the Antient and Royal Forest of Dartmoor* (1848), Samuel Rowe described the tors as 'Rock Idols', noting that many people believed them to be worshipped by the Druids. Captivated by their fantastical quality, he went into rhapsodies about them: 'Vast and gloomy castles appear to frown defiance from the beetling crags around. But no mortal hand ever laid their adamantine foundations, or reared their dizzy towers. Nature is the engineer that fortified the heights, thousands of years ago, - hers are the massive walls, hers the mighty bastions, hers the hand that reared those stupendous citadels which fable might have garrisoned with demigods and beleaguered with Titans…'

Roos Tor

The tors are compelling. There is something inherently fascinating about them. Although they are natural, we can't help seeing some as almost man-made, like sculptures. This is to some extent down to Modernist sculptors like Henry Moore and Barbara Hepworth who were so inspired by the tors and megaliths, and who became so popular, that we have inherited their vision of natural stone as art. They are often in unusual, flying and fantastical shapes, some of which appear like animals, faces, buildings and other dreamy imaginings. They have natural grandeur in scale and in the vistas they command. Their dramatic lines and angles often form rectangles and squares, again, giving them a constructed, otherworldly, almost alien air.

For thousands of years, myths and legends have grown up around the tors, and it is easy to see why. They fire the imagination. The first people to settle Dartmoor, around three to four thousand years ago in the Bronze Age, created stone monuments of circles and lines that responded to this rocky terrain; there is a strong suggestion that some of the monuments were positioned directly in relation to the tors which might also have been seen as worthy of worship, reverence or other form of deep connection in their own right. It certainly seems evident that these megalithic (and mini

Down Tor row, summer solstice

The hen of Hen Tor

The Thirlestone, Watern Tor

The Dewerstone (artist unknown) from *Picturesque England*, 1891

lithic) arrangements were sited with care, taking into consideration significant landscape features as well as the sea, the sun and the moon.

To state the obvious, the individual granite stones used in these megalithic ritual places are made out of the tors. So the stones brought the tors, and the granite landscape, into the centre of human life and death rituals. There also are a number of monuments across Dartmoor, for example the rare tor cairns and rarer ring cairns around tors, where the natural stone is the focus of the structure instead of the usual human burial. Maybe here the living stone was a vehicle for the dead, for example for excarnations (leaving bodies to decay naturally on the stone), or maybe the spirit of the stone was revered. Either way it gives us the sense that the stone is more a respected partner in these megalithic monuments, rather than an inert material to be built with. It is also suggestive of the importance of the stone itself that the megaliths on Dartmoor are hardly ever shaped by human hand; instead they are carefully selected for the natural form of the rock - tall, squared, pointed, curved, sparkling quartz or dark granite.

In more recent centuries, stories have grown up around certain tors. Take the Dewerstone for example (pictured left in a Victorian drawing). This is an enormous crag towering above the River Plym, supposedly the haunt of the Dewer, or Devil, who resides at the top of it. Also known as the Black Huntsman, he has a pack of black whist (meaning ghostly) hounds with whom he hunts human souls, often luring them to the top of the tor, and then sweeping them to their deaths below.

At least part of the tors' role in mythmaking is due to fundamental human psychology. We naturally seem to project human ideas and feelings onto other things around us. In the case of landscapes, we talk of them as human bodies: foothills, mountain spines, heads of valleys and mouths of rivers. We have a strong tendency to see meaningful images in natural patterns; psychologists call this pareidolia. This behaviour is part of our DNA: quick recognition of other humans and animals in the natural environment is an advantage to survival in the wild. The habit persists in the way we might suddenly see a human or animal face in a rock. And so stones have become the foundation of myths, a lithic carnival of giants, hunters, devils, dogs, ravens, eagles and spirits. Although we like to think we are telling stories about the stone, you could say the stones are telling our stories to us.

Certainly, with contemporary writers and artists, there is more of this sense that the stone is speaking to us, or we can have a dialogue with the land and its non-human parts. Groundbreaking artist Richard Long has created many of his walking artworks on Dartmoor, allowing the tors to shape his life path, literally and metaphorically. His work

English stonecrop

Sunburst' lichen

'Rock Foam' lichen

is imbued with the sense of deep time that starts to flow through those who spend their lives amongst the tors. In his 24-hour, 55-mile walk *Dartmoor Time* (1996) he describes:

'Holding a butterfly with a lifespan of one month, climbing over granite 350 million years old on Great Mis Tor, thinking of a future walk, eight hours of moonlight'

The tors are millions of years old; they are the serrated stumps of mountains. The process that started their formation began around 280 million years ago, in the Carboniferous period, when the earth's tectonic plates shifted, causing massive movement which resulted in rock melting deep inside the earth. The red-hot magma, in a plume called a batholith, pushed up in explosive volcanos through the sedimentary rocks above, before cooling to become high granite peaks. Then, over millions of years, the wear and tear of ice and water gradually exposed the granite, with chemical weathering and the severe climatic conditions of the Ice Ages resulting in the weird and wonderful shapes we see today.

There is no real agreement as to how many tors there are on Dartmoor. Estimates vary from around 150 to over 300, depending on your definition. What is certain is that they are the crowning glory of the moor, dotting and defining the landscape, making it unmistakeably 'Dartmoor'. The tors could also be said to be the base of the area's ecosystem, as the granite underneath defines what can live there. On the high moor, the granite pans retain water, creating bogs and peat and making the soil acidic in comparison to the protected limestone valleys on the outskirts where the lush semi-tropical rainforests form.

A fascinating natural world surrounds the tors which, although they may appear at first sight to be barren rock, support a fascinating spectrum of life. They provide shelter for blue beetles, hunting grounds for buzzards circling overhead, and even bird baths for ravens. Our particular obsession though is with the lichen which creates millions of miniature landscapes on the rocks, each one stranger than the last. A symbiotic combination of fungus and algae, lichens have fascinated storytellers and scientists alike with their weird biology as well as their uncanny shapes that reflect our own images and stories back to us, just like the faces in the tors. On Dartmoor we find many evocative lichen names: parts of the human body - *Porina chlorotica* - pale pimple lichen and *Parmelia omphalodes*, the navel lichen; real and fantastical creatures - *Cladonia pxydata* – pixy cup lichen, *Peltigera canina* - dog tooth lichens, *Cladonia squamosal* - dragon lichen; and even a lichen that tells its own stories - *Graphis scripta* which gets its name from its resemblance to secret writing.

The tors are natural focal points in Dartmoor's upland landscape, and ever since people started to walk for leisure and health purposes, back in the eighteenth century, 'tor bagging' has been popular, with people listing them, ranking them and rating them. Indeed, social media has only encouraged this trend, with groups avidly sharing their enthusiasm, as well as information about their discoveries. Letterboxing - where a box containing a notebook and a stamp is hidden for fellow walkers to find - started in the middle of the nineteenth century, invented by a moorland guide called James Perrott from Chagford, who placed the first one at Cranmere Pool. The craze continues today, with people visiting as many tors as they can as part of the process.

Many books have been written about Dartmoor in the last two hundred years, which still inform today's thinking about the tors. There are many we have used as reference points in this book. We've already mentioned Samuel Rowe's *A Perambulation of the Antient and Royal Forest of Dartmoor*, which was first published in 1848, and his description of

Bowerman's Nose, William Widgery

On the slopes of Dartmoor, artist unknown, *English Pictures*, 1885

the tors as 'rock idols'. In richly florid prose, Rowe relates his numerous and extensive excursions all over Dartmoor, done entirely on foot or horseback and without the benefits of modern technology.

His book contains beautiful illustrations, as did many of the guides written before the advent of photography. One of them, a drawing of the stone circle at Scorhill, by C F Williams, is on page 2. Artists were employed to draw Dartmoor's features, using a variety of techniques including wood cutting, line-engraving, and etching. These days, photography has pretty much taken over, but in our book, we pay homage to those early days of Dartmoor guides when the artists captured something of the feeling of the place as much as its appearance.

Another of our reference sources is one of the most famous: Crossing's *Guide to Dartmoor*, which was first published around 60 years later, in 1909. William Crossing was born in Plymouth in 1847, one year before Samuel Rowe's *Perambulation* came out. Brian Le Messurier, in the introduction to the 1965 reprint of the second, 1912 edition, describes it as a masterpiece and 'the best topographical book about Dartmoor that has ever been published', mainly, he says, 'because no other writer has explored the moor so extensively in all seasons and all weathers.'

Crossing has this to say about tors in the opening pages of the book: 'These granite masses, of which there are about 170 on Dartmoor, form one of its most striking features. The word is really from the Celtic twr, tower, and it not inaptly describes their appearance, for many of them rise to a considerable height above the ground. Usually they are seen crowning a hill, but this is not always the case.'

High Dartmoor by Eric Hemery, first published in 1983, is a massive tome of over 1000 pages which is so big it has to be contained in a box. It provides detailed descriptions of the features of Dartmoor, organised by the river valleys. At the beginning of the book, in a section entitled 'An

Dartmoor from *English Pictures* 1885 (artist unknown)

Vixen Tor, F J Widgery

Black faced sheep

Outline Biography of Dartmoor', he talks about the formation of the tors in the last Ice Age: 'During the glacials, ice attacked the granite peaks along their joints of weakness (mostly vertical or horizontal) so that they came to resemble castles under siege, transforming the skyline into one of magnificent, towering ruins…As the tors were being formed, granite blocks, many of immense size, were dislodged by the action of frost and ice from the tors to crash at their feet. The largest of these have remained to help us visualise the drama of their collapse; the rest became moving rivers of rocks …the process would then be repeated again and again until the hill slope became a veritable wilderness of boulders or clitter.'

A more recent book is Jeremy Butler's five-volume *Dartmoor Atlas of Antiquities*, published between 1991 and 1998 and sadly out of print. Jeremy, a dentist from Torquay, and passionate amateur archaeologist, produced this pioneering series of books after 20 years of research, including aerial and ground photography and surveys. The books are a comprehensive listing and description, with maps, of all of Dartmoor's historic sites. Jeremy, who also managed to gain a degree and a PhD in archaeology while practising as a dentist, was awarded the first-ever Dartmoor Society Award in 1998, in recognition of his work.

Much more recently, Josephine Collingwood's *Dartmoor Tors Compendium* (2018) is a striking photographic record of the tors, with stunning black and white imagery, as well as key geological facts about each stack.

These books have been hugely influential in forming perceptions of Dartmoor today, and there is much ongoing work, research and online discussion on the subject. There are some very good websites; Tim Sandles' fascinating *Legendary Dartmoor* is strong on history and folklore, backed up with old documents and records that shed light on Dartmoor's past. Another excellent resource is the archive of a small charity called the Dartmoor Trust. This is an online collection of thousands of photographs, video and audio recordings that record the history of Dartmoor and its people. *The Tors of Dartmoor* website by Tim Jenkinson, Max Piper and Paul Buck, has a wealth of information and photographs, as well as some evocative descriptions. *Dartmoor Explorations* by Steve Grigg and *Prehistoric Dartmoor Walks* by Dave Parks are also both highly recommended.

Dartmoor is enjoyed by many thousands of visitors and locals every year. Recently, it has become the focus of a national campaign calling for greater public access to open spaces, with protest marches focussing on Stall Moor, where a landowner has challenged the right to wild camp without permission. Passions have been aroused because residents and visitors alike care very deeply about this place.

We share this passion and *Rock Idols* is, quite simply, a love letter to the tors, extraordinary natural forms, some of which have been shaped by humans in the recent past but which have been shaping us over many millennia. We have selected the tors that speak to us, and our book is an attempt to convey their magic, tell some stories about them, both personal and legendary, and also to understand why they make us feel the way they do, and why they have such universal appeal. We think that by looking at the individual tors and trying to listen

Right to wild camp demo, Hound Tor October 2024

The Pulpit' cairn circle

to what they have to tell us, we can tell a story of Dartmoor, both past and present. The book also has some of the practical information you need to find the tors for yourself, although we always recommend using the Ordnance Survey map as well. Many tors are in remote locations, frequently affected by bad weather, and only reachable over rough and wet terrain, so all walks need proper preparation and kit.

On a personal level, Dartmoor has huge emotional resonance for us. In 2017 our elder son Felix died suddenly and unexpectedly. His death changed our lives completely, and since this huge loss, we have come to find great solace in the ebb and flow of life on the moor and our growing connection to the deep time of Dartmoor, and, in particular, the tors. As his life was intertwined with these stones, so they hold the memory of him and all of our ancestors, witnessing the sparks of our lives flicker in front of them and comforting us with reminders that they, as we, are just part of the constant motion of the earth, land and stones.

It is the sense of motion, liveliness and life in the stone that we have tried to capture in the art and writing in this book. People talk about stone as inanimate and cold; having a 'heart of stone' means to be dead inside. On the contrary, stone is most definitely 'alive', just on a different timescale, rising as magma, cooling, fracturing, falling, ground down by water and ice, sedimented and ultimately subducted back into the earth's core. Dartmoor granite, which seems inert on the surface, also has a secret beating heart of uranium and thorium, their radioactive decay marking off deep time with the precision of an atomic clock.

We hope then you enjoy with us both the small moments on the tors; granite beneath the feet, rain on the face, lichen crisp to the touch, as well as the exhilarating views from the top, the great blue distances between tors and the even greater eons of time stretching both backwards and forwards from these magical summits.

GOOD TO KNOW

CONTENT: We have ordered the chapters in the sequence we visited these particular tors, from the winter of early 2024 through to the autumn of that year. Each chapter contains a detailed description of the tor and what you can see around it, as well as an account of our expedition there. We also provide information on where to park and the basic route to walk, but you will need to use a map to navigate as well. There is more practical information about access land and safety at the back of the book.

MAP REFERENCES: At the end of each chapter, you will find location references for the tor and the features around it. We have given three types: GPS coordinates, OS grid references and What3Words locations. We have used the 1967 Ordnance Survey Dartmoor tourist map by way of illustration, as it is a thing of beauty and is out of copyright.

TOR NAMES: Many of the tors have more than one name and spelling, leading, in some cases, to quite intense debate. There are many reasons for this, but, for simplicity, we have chosen to use the name that is used on the Ordnance Survey map. We realise that other names are often used which may be just as valid.

CLITTER, KISTS AND CAIRNS: There is quite a lot of terminology for the features on Dartmoor which we have compiled into a glossary at the back of the book. In particular, the word Kist, short for Kistvaen, can be spelled with either a C or a K. We have chosen to use K because this is the traditional spelling of the word in Devon.

Image opposite: East Mill Tor by Alex Murdin

GREATOR ROCKS

'Rising from the April bluebell carpet in the unusual form of vertical, compressed, sheet-like masses – weird of form in mist – is Greator Rocks or Grea Tor (1,150 feet); characterising the romantic exaggeration so often expressed by early Victorian painters of hill-country scenes, it is, for good measure, backed by that remarkable fortress of Nature, Great Hound Tor.'

Eric Hemery, *High Dartmoor,* 1983

Dartmoor is all about dirt and drama, mud and magic. We feel this was somehow encapsulated in our first tour of tors for *Rock Idols*, when we set out to visit Greator Rocks on a very cold, still, winter day. We had stopped off at the local agricultural merchants on an industrial estate off the dual-carriage way, after manure for the veg patch (they had run out). Soon though we left the refrigerator suppliers and packaging manufacturers behind as we entered the deep winding lanes leading to the moor. Then, as we approached Trendlebeare Down, a buzzard floated across the front of the car, a frozen and fleeting moment of great detail, with its looming bulk, yellow stockinged and fan-tailed, a moment of pure joy.

We reached Manaton and headed south along single-track, potholed lanes, passing a large hand-written sign saying ICE: ROAD IMPASSABLE. In the wintery sunshine, on a clear road surrounded by green fields, we took it for an old notice and carried on, but after about 5 minutes we found ourselves on a terrifying uphill ice rink, with the road covered in ice at least an inch thick. Fortunately, it had partly melted on the left-hand side, so with 2 wheels with some traction, and a foot to the floor, it was a tense few minutes as we drove up the hill. We were relieved to get to Hound Tor car park at the top in one piece.

Greator Rocks – or as it used to be called – Grea Tor – occupies a commanding position overlooking the Becka Brook valley (also known as Hound Tor Combe), with views over towards Haytor, Holwell Tor, Saddle Tor and Rippon Tor. It has a fairytale air, because of its tower-like columns of rock, which, from the southern side, appear like battlements, and also because of a cave that is twice the height of the average person. This is known sometimes as 'the Hermits Cave', and has a huge horizontal rock over the entrance, like a lintel, reminding one of a dolmen, a prehistoric burial tomb like the one called Spinsters Rock, not far away near Chagford. It is quite surprising that none of the main Dartmoor books mention it, as it is perhaps Greator Rocks' most unusual feature. Most tors have some holes and crevices, even tunnels, but a shelter like this that you can stand up in is quite exceptional. There is also a strange boulder at the bottom of the tor on the southern side, with what appear to be linear carvings on it, which, again, we cannot find referenced anywhere in the Dartmoor guides.

Greator Rocks is also close to some fascinating features, most notably the remains of a medieval village, which was excavated in the 1960s by a team of volunteers led by Marie Minter, a pioneering female archaeologist from Torquay. There is a wonderful film about this dig, complete with re-enactments, that you can currently watch on Dartmoor National Park's website.

From the car park, we slithered down the icy

Remains of the medieval village

road on foot, before turning off at a cattlegrid and walking up past the eastern side of Hound Tor. Everyone knows about the medieval village near Hound Tor, but we had read (in Jeremy Butler's *Dartmoor Atlas of Antiquities*) about another medieval ruin - part of the same settlement - to the north of it. After consulting the maps in both Butler and the Ordnance Survey, we found it a short distance off the main path; quite overgrown but still visible. There was one fairly substantial building with a room for the humans at one end, and another smaller building, which, according to Butler, was a barn. Wandering around exploring, we were struck by the way the ruins were framed by a trio of trees higher up the hill, a winter trinity of an oak, a holly and a rowan, with Hound Tor towering above.

We carried on towards the main medieval village, passing a large, twisted oak tree growing at the top of a slope. It looked like Medusa's head, with numerous moss-covered boughs snaking out from its central trunk. Dripping with lichens, and surrounded by mossy boulders, it was a fantastically rich sight in this grey winter setting.

Once we got to the medieval village, the ruins, surrounded by flat grass as though in a municipal park, seemed manicured and almost sterile in comparison to the ones we'd just visited. However this meant the outlines of the buildings were clear, and it wasn't hard to imagine this place 800 years earlier, as thatched houses and barns, with smoke drifting from the roofs, and the sounds of people talking and working in the small fields that surrounded the village. Great Tor Rocks with its two main peaks and a third pile of rocks to the side, reared up very close by, and we thought of the village children, who would have had the tor, and in particular its cave, as their playground.

It's thought the area was first used by shepherds and cattle farmers in the 11th and 12th centuries

Recent rock art

for summer pasture; they built huts as shelters. These shelters then evolved into a small farming hamlet around 1200; records show that one of the first lords of the manor was a Richard de Hundetorra. Altogether there were probably about 20 or 30 villagers, who farmed about 10 acres of arable fields around the village. The archaeology shows three main longhouses where both animals and humans lived, as well as the remains of barns with kilns where the oats and rye they grew were dried. The village seems to have died out by the end of the 14th century, succumbing to climate change in the form of dropping temperatures and increased rainfall, as well as a global pandemic, the Black Death.

We left the village and approached the tor from the northern side. Despite it being the middle of winter, it appeared lustrous and full of life, with masses of plants growing out of its cracks. Bilberry, gorse, ivy, heather, pennywort and moss covered the rocks, and trees including hollies and rowans were growing out of the crevices. We climbed up through a dip in between the two main peaks, to find the cave secreted on the other side, like a hermit's retreat. Inside we discovered a drawing of a labyrinth on one of the walls. Next to it were the remains of another image, but much of it was obscured; a friend tells us she has heard these were created in the last decade; the other drawing apparently was of a horned cow or bull. As we stood looking at the white lines of the labyrinth, we wondered who had drawn it, and why. There is much speculation about the meaning of this symbol, with suggestions, for example, that it represents the soul's journey into the underworld, or that it is a metaphor for our path through life, or that it represents Mother Earth. Others believe it to be a fertility symbol that was used in pagan rituals. What is certain is that this cave, like a womb in this edifice of rock, feels like a special place.

Leaving the cave, we climbed down to the southern side of the tor, where fingers of rock grasped skywards. The dominant impression was of wild verticality, huge pinnacles of rock thrusting upwards. Marvelling at the views above us, we then noticed a large boulder at the bottom of the tor, with angular lines carved into it. The carvings looked man-made, but by whom, and when? The rock was

Pennywort

also covered by a dark colour which looked a bit like soot or the remains of a fire. Maybe someone, inspired by the labyrinth in the cave, felt the same desire to mark the landscape? Or perhaps the other way round, are these ancient Neolithic markings which were spotted by the labyrinth makers?

We continued to walk around the eastern end of the tor which was much softer and more rounded than the starker, southern side. After doing the full circuit, we set off back towards the car park, admiring the soaring flanks of Hound Tor, the black dogs in full flight on its south-western side. One more treat awaited us; a glorious cairn circle and kistvaen dating back around three thousand years to Bronze Age times. This is an ancient place of burial, a prehistoric ritual monument where flesh was consigned to the earth.

We walked around the circle of large kerb stones surrounding the kist, although on one side there were quite a few missing; likely plundered at some stage in the past for other purposes like road mending. In the centre was the kist, or stone chest, in which the ashes or bones of the deceased would have been placed. Originally, stones and earth would have been piled on top, to form a barrow, a dark mound in front of the looming mass of Hound Tor, whose dog stones guard it. Something of this is captured in a delicately atmospheric lithograph of it by Charles Frederick Williams in Samuel Rowe's *Perambulation of Dartmoor*, (pictured below). These ancient features, the prehistoric cairn circle, and the medieval village, resurrected in our minds the people who lived here many centuries before us. They would have known these tors around them intimately. Greator Rocks, in comforting familiarity and granite inhumanity, would have been part of their sense of rootedness to this place, in both life and death.

INFORMATION

GREATOR ROCKS:
50.5937, -3.7711, SX 74739 78639,
What3Words: euphoric.vivid.posts

ALSO OF INTEREST:
Medieval village: 50.5952, -3.7723, SX 74652 78787, What3Words: subsystem.fractions.speaker
Cave at Great Tor Rocks: 50.5938, -3.7707, SX 74765 78622, What3words: gagging.shimmered.disputes
Cairn circle and kist: 50.594, -3.7801, SX 74101 78765, What3Words: mermaids.finer.swinging
Possible incised boulder: 50.5938, -3.7700, SX 74813 78619, What3Words: glimmers.obstinate.swan

ACCESS:
You can park at Hound Tor car park (What3words: insurance.postcard.headrest). From here walk east over Hound Tor and down to the medieval village before heading south to Greator Rocks. From here you can walk north-west in a circle back to the car, passing the ancient kist and circle on the way. Alternatively, you can park by Holwell Lawn (What3Words: less.swatted.obtain) and walk north-east through the Pony Club land at Holwell Lawn to find Greator Rocks. This is a particularly nice route at bluebell time.

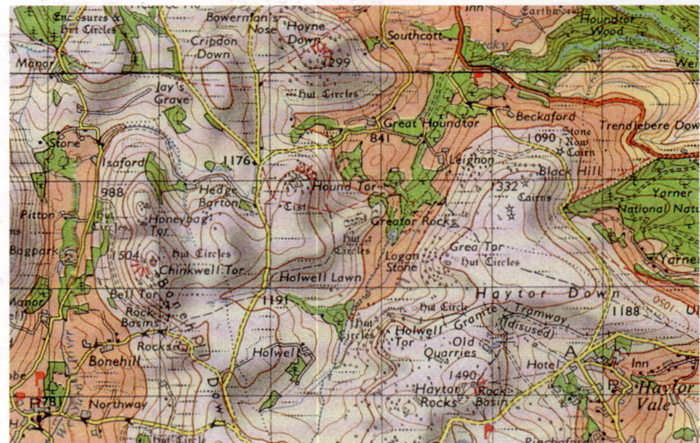

Possible inscribed stone

BENCH TOR

'Rendered as Benjay Tor on the first edition of the OS one-inch map of 1809, the tor consists of several piles on an elongated promontory... The two principal ones North Tor and South Tor, afford impressive views of the mountain river five hundred feet below about to quit its birthland, as well as an audible appreciation of its force and current. One of the smaller piles was once known as Eagle Rock – as also was the summit of Looka Tor (Luckey Tor) on the valley floor – and there can be little doubt that the solitude and awesome nature of the scenery in the vicinity of both tors made them an ideal habitat for the golden eagle before men drove him into the fastnesses of northern Scotland.'

Eric Hemery, *High Dartmoor,* 1983

It was freezing cold in our temperature-inverted river valley on the edge of Dartmoor, but golden light touched the hilltops as we left the house one January morning. Temperatures the previous night had fallen to minus 7 degrees and everywhere was white with frost.

The intention had been to visit Crockern Tor, but just a mile into the journey, following the misty form of the River Dart, we encountered a scarlet ROAD CLOSED sign, with no indication of where the road closure was located. Undeterred, we carried on, but then lost our nerve as we encountered another closure sign at the next junction. Given that the route is just one of two across the moor -and worried about black ice on a diversion down narrow lanes - we decided to visit an old friend instead.

Bench Tor looms over the Dart Gorge, the river carving its way through the valley below. It is one of those places that is deeply familiar to us; just a few miles from our home, we've visited it regularly over the last twenty years, often with our sons, from when they were quite small, spending happy days running around enthusiastically in their wellies. The lumpy granite and grass playground provided all the nooks and crannies needed. They used to hide in the black fissures and jump out from behind stone stacks. In their teenage years, it was different, with more background static about being dragged out into the great outdoors.

Unlike most tors, Bench Tor does not crown the summit of a hill but is spread out along a ridge, in a series of outcrops like a giant's stepping stones. What is most interesting about it is that it is defined more by the enormous void alongside it, than by its positive presence. This void is the Dart Gorge where a gouged arc of millions of tons of stone has been cracked, then washed and rounded, pulverised into clay and gravel and dispatched eastwards towards the sea.

We drove onto the high moor, expecting to see a glittering white winterscape, but were surprised to see that all the frost had melted away, as the dawn had risen earlier on this upland shelf of moorland. The sun was so bright, the scene, in a bizarre way,

Looking down into the Dart Gorge

felt like a petrified summer. Perhaps, due to recent tree felling, there was more light being reflected off the silver disc of Venford Reservoir, a short distance from the tor. Hundreds of conifers have been removed in recent months, and the still, mirrored water was visible from afar. We remembered the trees before their fall. When the water's surface was completely still like this, they were perfectly reflected in the water, a mirrored acoustic-shaped wave of blue-green needles.

Walking north from the reservoir, we reached the first outcrop and became enveloped by the constant white noise of the river rushing up from the River Dart below, a dominant sound on this windless day. Over this background noise we heard the drone of an aeroplane propeller, a small grey frame flying along the course of the Dart below us, making the empty void of the valley seem even deeper. We came across a fellow walker in a crimson jacket sitting against a rock, soaking up the sun and having a drink from his flask. His name was Peter Hughes. 'The tors are focal points to aim for', he told us. 'They are easily identifiable landmarks, sort of reference points for your walk. Bench Tor is one of my favourites because you do feel as though you are on a precipice, there is a great sense of height. One of my New Year's resolutions is to learn and memorise all the names of the tors, as I can never remember them, and they are such wonderful markers in the landscape.'

We bid Peter goodbye and meandered north, enjoying the easy ridge walk over smooth grey granite and rabbit-cropped turf; a very different experience from visiting most tors, where you have to scramble up and clamber around towering blocks. We passed a small cliff on the eastern side with a canopy of thick ivy, like an awning protruding over a shop. Unusually, the ivy was

supported on a network of thick branches growing away from the rock, rather than clinging to it. There were some deep earthy crevices underneath, and it felt like an intimate domestic scene, a smaller, friendlier part of the tor. It was somewhere our sons used to like to play.

We reached the end of the tor which flies, buttress-like, above the Dart Gorge, visible from Sharrah Pool in the Dart below. We admired the deep valley sides cloaked in the purple tips of the silver birch and the branches of oak covered in pastel-green lichens, the straggly Old Man's Beard and starbursts of Witches Whiskers. In previous times, the northern and southern ends of the tors were named individually, but today this seems to have disappeared: there is no reference to North Bench Tor and South Bench Tor on maps, and the location of 'Eagle Rock' which is also mentioned in the literature, has also faded into the mists of time. We tried to work out which of the various outcrops could be Eagle Rock, but we couldn't be sure. This

Venford Reservoir, before the trees were felled

tor would certainly be the perfect vantage point for any great bird of prey. Sitting on a large flat rock and enjoying the increasing warmth of the sun, we heard a whirring sound and a grey military helicopter flew overhead, another acoustic layer meshing with the faint river's roar.

It is the depth of space in front and below in combination with the extended views to the far undulating horizons that is breath-taking here: south, to Snowdon and Ryders' Hill, west, to North Hessary Tor and, swinging north and east, taking in Great Mis, Beardown, Longaford, Bellever, Yar and Corndon tors, then coming to rest on the spiralling snail shell swirls of Haytor's twin peaks. To walk along Bench Tor with the Dart raging below is to truly appreciate the magnificence of Dartmoor.

We looked across to the other side of the river, where several tors stood sentinel over the water. Sharp Tor, a beautiful pyramid as seen from Bench Tor, was the most noticeable and impressive. Below it, to the left, we spotted two dwellings: the one nearer Sharp Tor, with a red tile roof, was Rowbrook House, an arts and crafts building, while to its left was the humbler Rowbrook Farm. The latter is home to one of Dartmoor's most famous legends: that of Jan Coo, a farmhand who worked at Rowbrook, who kept running down to the River Dart below because he could hear someone calling. On the final occasion he never returned, and was assumed to have been abducted by the piskies or perhaps drowned, another victim of the river which claims a heart each year.

Scrambling down through the treeline of oaks on the sheltered eastern side of the tor, we found a different perspective entirely. Here were great stores of latent energy. Massive rocks had thrown themselves over the tor's edge and down the nearly vertical hillside, arrested at the last minute in their dramatic fall towards the river by other rocks and trees, but facing the inevitability of gravity and time. As we climbed back up again, the tor's movement inverted: grand columns of rock striking skywards, riven both horizontally and vertically.

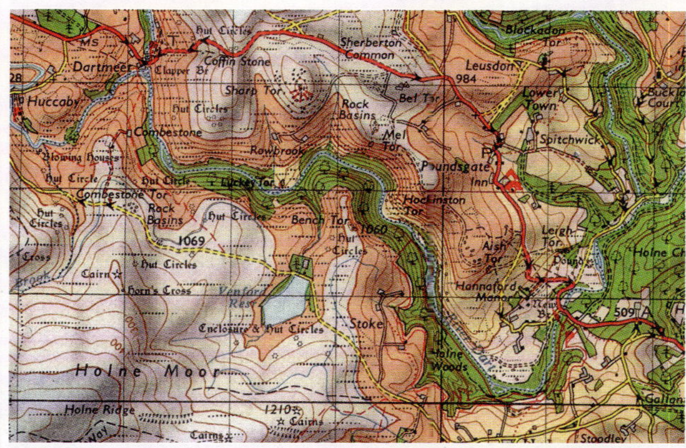

BENCH TOR:
50.5322, -3.8486, SX 69079 71909, What3Words: spades.quietest.strides

ALSO OF INTEREST:
Venford Reservoir: 50.5243, -3.8553, SX 68583 71043, What3Words: pulsing.scatters.draw

ACCESS:
There is a car park on the eastern side of Venford Reservoir (What3Words: typically.conveys.starlight). From here follow the footpaths (there are several) north-east for about half a mile until you reach Bench Tor.

MEL TOR

'It was at Mel Tor that the youth of Leusdon, many of them young farmers with an old-fashioned zest for making their own pleasures, revived the ceremony of wheel rolling. On 23rd June 1954, the Eve of St John the Baptist's Day, they sent a great wheel crashing down Mel Tor: a version of the European custom of rolling a burning wheel towards a stream. If the wheel reached the water the harvest would be good; if it became entangled in undergrowth, the harvest would be poor. The ceremony had lapsed for about a hundred years before this revival.'

Vian Smith, *Portrait of Dartmoor*, 1966

Mel Tor occupies a commanding position over the Dart Gorge, directly opposite Bench Tor, which it overlooks, being some 30 metres higher. The views from here are breathtaking: Venford Reservoir, over to the south, looks like a vast mirror on a still day. The tor sprawls over a large area and has several substantial outlying piles of rocks. Although today it is known as Mel Tor, Eric Hemery, in *High Dartmoor*, refers to it as Mil Tor, saying that "Mil" refers to 'middle' – this tor being between, he says, Sharp and Bel Tors. Looking at the modern map though, it would appear that Mel Tor is roughly in the middle of a triangle made by Sharp, Bel and Hockinston Tors.

It was a bitter, grey January day, the tail end of an unusually cold spell of weather, when we set off to visit the tor, one of our regular haunts. We hiked up the hill from the car park to get to Dr Blackall's Drive, which runs along the top of the hillside, teetering over the River Dart. Mel Tor is at the other end. This track was created in the 1880s by Dr Thomas Blackall, who practised medicine in Exeter but who also owned nearby Spitchwick Manor, which was his weekend retreat. He wanted to be able to ride along the top of the Dart Gorge in his carriage, and enjoy the views; hence his creation of a special driveway. As we walked along the track, gazing at the majestic views down to the river and across to the moor on the other side, we marvelled at the vision of our Victorian ancestors like Dr Blackall, who had no hesitation in putting their grand ideas into practice.

Down below us the woods appeared in muted shades of brown, grey and burgundy, and gorse surrounded us on both sides of the track, a dull green with ever-present yellow flowers smelling of coconut. We could see the white waters of the Dart foaming below, and then the dark oval of Sharrah Pool. How many times have we walked along that river, and swum in its beautiful waters? We've lost count, but it is a place that has accompanied us through thick and thin during the last two decades, its waters singing in the background like a Greek chorus.

We crunched through patches of ice, before reaching Brake Corner, presumably named because Dr Blackall's carriage would have had to slow down

here to avoid coming a cropper. Interestingly though, brake is also an old word for bracken, hence also thicket, rough or marshy overgrown land, which could well apply here. Holly trees and hawthorn trees stood like lollipops in the landscape, the hawthorns festooned with delicate olive-grey Usnea lichen hanging in swathes from their branches. We could see Mel Tor looming in the distance, and took a small path off the main track towards it, passing a large and interesting outcrop we call 'Jesus' Tomb'. This is a substantial distance to the south-east of the main group and is dominated by an enormous flat rock on its side, like the stone across the cave where Christ was buried in the Bible stories. Behind it is a hollow space, a sepulchre, into which we could have climbed if we'd been inclined to squeeze through a gap beside the massive cold slab.

Moving on from the outcrop and approaching the main mass of Mel Tor, we saw a flash of orange up ahead. Momentarily confused, we wondered what on earth it could be. Then we saw it again, a dog fox with a big bushy tail, loping around the rocks ahead of us, before disappearing off to the right.

We think of Mel Tor as 'the tor of circles'. As well as the round stone at Jesus' Tomb, there are rock basins on its summit, an abandoned half-carved millstone at its foot, and even a story involving flaming cartwheels. The rock basins are its most famous feature. For centuries these hollows, which can be found on some tors but not others, were thought to have been the work of the Druids. Theories varied wildly; some thought they were created to collect water for ritual purification practices, in which sacred plants like mistletoe or oak would be infused. Others believed them to be receptacles for the blood from human sacrifices. No less wondrous is the geological explanation, that these are created by the microcosmic battle between water and granite in a glacially slow process that started 71,000 years ago in the Devensian Ice Ages. In other words, they are natural features, created by erosion and weathering.

As we approached the tor from the south-west we gravitated towards one of our favourite parts: an outcrop on the left which protrudes precariously over the rocks below. It appears variously like a gentleman's flat cap, or a whale rising from the depths, or even a bemittened hand pointing down to the river below. We found the half-complete millstone nearby, on the southern side. According to the *Tors of Dartmoor* website, 'its abandonment (is) indicative of stone cutting on the tor in times gone by'. Someone decided to take a chisel to one of the rocks to make a millstone, but then gave up.

The wind was starting to get stronger and felt quite bitter, but we wanted to see the rock basins so braved the climb up to the top of the highest part of the tor. There they were, small but distinct, but we were keen to get out of the icy wind and so climbed down hastily. From here we headed

Abandoned millstone

Tor granite with quartz veins

Rock basins

around to the western side to find a series of small cliffs surrounded by rocks littered below, many at strange angles, which looked as though they'd just fallen there yesterday. This side of the tor felt vital, alive, urgent, chaotic, despite being solid and unmoving; we felt a palpable sense of connection to deep time in motion, to something much older and more profound than ourselves.

The wind was howling by now and we moved around the tor to shelter in a nook on its eastern side, looking down to the River Dart roaring below. Mel Tor was the scene of an unusual custom which died out sometime in the last century, where villagers would roll wagon wheels down the hill towards the river. Further research by the *Tors of Dartmoor* website suggests that the wheels would have been packed with straw and set alight; if they went out before they reached the river that would indicate a poor harvest; if they made it to the river still ablaze, a good harvest would ensue. It would certainly have made quite a spectacle, but it seems incredible, given the massive blocks of stone and trees everywhere, that the cartwheels could have built up enough speed to make it down to the river without falling over? It is likely there were fewer trees then but perhaps they built special runs, plotted angles and ramps, did trick shots…

As we sat there thinking about this long-lost tradition, a penny dropped. We've twice found old iron-clad cartwheels while swimming in the Dart. Both times we found them much further downstream, near Ashburton, and at the time we found it extraordinary; how on earth had they ended up there? But maybe the old custom explains why. Perhaps, many decades ago, they'd been rolled down the hill from Mel Tor. They may have spent years on the forest floor before ending up in the river. Over decades, they would have moved downstream…until we found them. Maybe others will have continued all the way down the Dart to Dartmouth, and out into the open sea. This wheel's on fire, rolling down the road…

The Western cliff

MEL TOR:
50.5384, -3.8448, SX 69353 72579, What3Words: producing.meaty.forever

ALSO OF INTEREST:
'Jesus's Tomb': 50.5374, -3.8434, SX 69464 72479, What3Words: butterfly.output.removable
Rock basins on the summit of the tor: 50.5384, -3.8448, SX 69361 72590, What3Words: tapes.relations.sketch
A possible abandoned millstone: 50.5379, -3.845, SX 69345 72539, What32words: acoustics.movie.revival

ACCESS:
Bel Tor car park is the nearest (What3words: jars.series.joys). Walk south from the car park until you reach a track where you turn left. Follow the track as it bends to the south and takes you to Mel Tor, a walk of about 0.5 miles. A more scenic walk to the tor is from Dr Blackalls Drive car park (What3Words: keyboards.clipped.button). From there walk uphill to pick up Dr Blackalls Drive which takes you north-west to Mel Tor, a walk of about 1.5 miles.

Jesus' Tomb

THE DEWERSTONE

'This huge mass of rock rises perpendicularly from the margin of the stream to an immense height. Its whole surface is jagged and seamed in the manner so peculiar to granite.... numerous hawks, ravens &c may be seen floating around its rugged crest and filling the air with their hoarse screamings....The rocks immediately beneath the view seem as if they had been struck at once by a thousand thunderbolts...'

N T Carrington, *Dartmoor: A Descriptive Poem,* (actually a note within the book, written by his son Henry Carrington) 1826

The Dewerstone is one of the better-known tors of Dartmoor; a picturesque etching of it forms the frontispiece of *Dartmoor: A Descriptive Poem*, by romantic poet N T Carrington, which was published in 1826 (see page 41). The drawing by Plymouth-based, self-described 'Cattle, Landscape & Portrait Painter' Philip Hutchins Rogers, shows stark and jagged rocks barren of trees, which is not the case today. It is best visited in the winter months, as in the summer much of this extraordinary rock is hidden behind foliage.

It is a truly gothic edifice. Great columns of stone, like buttresses, tower around 160 metres over the River Plym which thunders along below. Its natural drama has made it ripe for legends, the most famous of which is about the Devil – 'Dewer' in the Devon dialect - who lures hapless travellers to the top, before sweeping them over the edge into the slavering jaws of his terrifying pack of black dogs, the whisht hounds, which wait at the bottom. Eric Hemery, writing in *High Dartmoor* in 1983, says this legend is '...almost credible, especially when the sun is setting blood-red behind Roborough Down on a wild November afternoon and a swirling mist wreaths crags and treetops.'

The Dewerstone maintains its cloak of mystery and elusiveness today as the lush Devon rainforest that envelops it makes it nigh on impossible to get a complete view of it at any one time. The best way to admire its setting is to approach from the opposite side of the river, starting at Cadover Bridge. This is what we decided to do on a dank February morning of dense Dartmoor mists. It was one of those winter days when, even though it's not raining hard, the dampness and murk seem to penetrate your every bone.

We rolled up at the car park, which resembled Swiss cheese, it had so many potholes. Setting off west along the path above the River Plym, we followed an old pipeline through North Wood which was used to transport liquid china clay from where it was mined, higher up on the moor, down to the gigantic settling tanks at Shaugh Bridge in the valley below. Oak trees surrounded us, their trunks covered in acid-green Rough-stalked

Feather-mosses, surprisingly luminous in this dark winter scene. Down below, the peaty river churned and gurgled down cascades and pools, and the path gradually started to ascend, leaving the river behind.

We were surprised by how much of the pipeline has survived. Most of it is made of glazed earthenware ceramic, but there were also some sections made of iron. Every so often we would pass large stone boxes by the side of the path. According to the *Dartmoor Explorations* website, these are inspection chambers, used to access the pipe, especially if the workers had to sort out blockages. Much of the path was squelchy and white, indicative of the clay still present in the ground.

Looking across to the other side of the valley, in the hope of glimpsing the Dewerstone, we had to be patient; it turned out to be further along than we had thought. Eventually, the first magnificent buttress came into view, protruding from the hillside, surrounded by the greeny-grey skeletons of trees, covered with lichens. Then, a little further along, more crags appeared and then disappeared, revealed and then hidden by dense swirls of mist floating up the valley. As we descended towards the river, the sight of the rock was lost to us altogether.

We arrived at Shaugh Bridge, where there is a car park and the remains of the clay works: the loading bays are still quite intact. Once over the river, we started to climb up a distinctive, wide paved path, which felt rather like the famous yellow brick road in *The Wizard of Oz*, purposefully forging ahead through the trees. Although it was the middle of winter, the woods still wore clothes of green; lichen and moss were everywhere. An army type ran past us with an enormous backpack, obviously in training for some sort of physical challenge. As we trudged up the steep hill, he passed us several times, up and down. Eventually, out of breath, we arrived at what felt like the top of the Dewerstone, although it was actually just the top of one particular cliff. A huge vertical crack down one side gave the impression of the rock being about to split open at any moment.

The tor stretches from the bottom of the valley near the river, up the wooded hillside, with another, final outcrop at the top on the open moor. Its huge, looming mass, with sheer walls of rock, is irresistible to climbers. They have come up with a whole series of tribal names for the many and varied routes, including the Cretin's Cavort, the Energy

Dewerstone by P H Rogers from
Dartmoor a Descriptive Poem by N T Carrington 1826

Crisis, the Cadbury's Flake, the Hagar the Horrible and the Twittering Crack.

Eric Hemery (*High Dartmoor, 1983*) has a wonderful story about one such climber, Michael Rabley, who was ascending a nearby crag called Crow's Buttress in 1960. He found a Bronze Age pottery cup, secreted on a ledge within a crevice, that had lug handles and surface decoration. It is now in the museum at Plymouth. There is further evidence of people living here in Neolithic times: on the open ground at the top of the Dewerstone, next to the top of the tor, are the remains of a small settlement dating back about three thousand years. Still very much visible is a large defensive double wall and ditch. There are a few hut circles (the stone remnants of thatched round houses) that show the place was occupied, but there is still a lot of speculation about the uses of these enclosures at the top of tors. It could have been a village, a meeting place, a fortification, a livestock corral, or even a place for ritual.

We sat on a flat boulder and ate our lunch, looking out over towards the trees on the other side of the valley and occasionally risking a look down below – not for the faint-hearted. We could hear the sound of voices and then caught a glimpse of some red and yellow rope, and a man appeared at the top of the rock from the other side. We thought about the climber who found the ancient beaker here over six decades ago. How exciting must that have been for him! And how on earth had it ended up there? Had it been deliberately placed on this lofty crag by one of the hilltop dwellers thousands of years ago with the cremated remains of their loved one inside, or maybe they were hiding a precious possession from marauders?

We girded our loins for the final, almost vertical, ascent up out of the trees to the top of the

Dewerstone on the open moor. Some call this outcrop Devil's Rocks. There is a simple memorial stone to the poet N T Carrington here, who was born in Plymouth in 1777 and died in Bath in 1830. He is most famous for his epic narrative work, *Dartmoor: A Descriptive Poem* published in 1826, derided and loved in equal measure for its passionate and fantastical portrait of Dartmoor.

It was tough going, and as we left the woods behind us an eerie mist descended, shrouding the summit. We wanted to find the memorial, which we knew was carved somewhere on the rocks. Eventually, we found Carrington's name, roughly incised into a flat boulder on the tor itself; the lettering is now quite faded but was still a thrill to make this connection to the famous poet, a bard of Dartmoor in this ghostly place.

It was a dewy and dim walk back through the silent grey clouds along the top of Wigford Down, back in a circle down to Cadover Bridge. As we reached our destination, a medieval cross (thought to have been erected by the monks of Plympton Priory to mark their route to Tavistock) loomed out of the mist as a final blessing to our romantic pilgrimage.

INFORMATION

DEWERSTONE:
50.4550, -4.0598 SX 53891 63794
What3Words: grace.roof.await
ALSO OF INTEREST:
Devil's Rocks: SX 53784 63897
What3Words: prices.worked.stages
Carrington memorial stone:
SX 53781 63896 What3words:
limes.upon.polite
Remains of China clay works:
SX 53344 63626 What3words:
lucky.frog.among
ACCESS:
The nearest car park is at Shaugh Bridge: 50.454, -4.0672 SX 53344 63626 What3words: lucky.frog.among. From the car park, cross the river and turn right. You can walk along the river to reach the bottom of the Dewerstone, or else take the paved path up to the top. For a longer walk, and to see the tor in its setting, park at Cadover Bridge 50.4624, -4.0381 SX 55430 64512 What 3 words: skin.polices.recount and follow the path west along the river to Shaugh Bridge and follow the directions above.

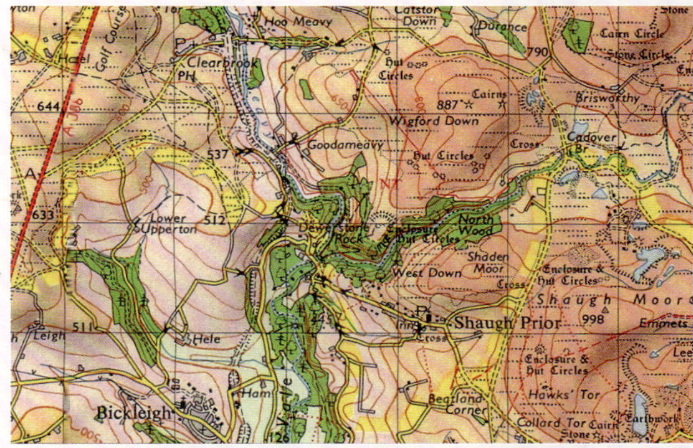

WEST MILL TOR

'The central pile has some notable features: a weathered rock face on the east side resembles that of Winter Tor; the west side is a dramatic ruin; the north-east portion of the pile consists of a large, court-like clearing under the shadow of a vast and rugged 'wing-wall', and north of this are several detached piles – two of them large – and other scattered ones beyond. The entire moorscape, with Yes Tor superior and aloof in the south-west... is very fine.'

Eric Hemery, *High Dartmoor,* 1983

West Mill Tor stands on the northern edge of Dartmoor, in the heart of the Okehampton firing range. Just to the north is Okehampton Camp, and all around is evidence of army activity, from spent small arms shells on the grass to abandoned concrete bunkers and shooting ranges. The Army has used Dartmoor for training for over 200 years and is still active here today.

West Mill Tor, like many tors, looks different according to which direction it's approached from. Seen from the south, it towers like a black fortification, dominant over all it surveys. Approaching from the east, it is defended by a granite tide of broken clitter, sharp-angled rocks that shut down any quick traverse. At the top, there are breathtaking views. Yes Tor and High Willhays sit to the south-west and Rowtor, Belstone and Winter Tors to the east; together they form a kind of bulwark, the northern-most defence of the high Dartmoor plateau which overlooks the farms of Mid and North Devon, all the way to the Bristol Channel.

It was a still, March morning as we drove onto the moor from Okehampton, up to the camp which guards the entrance to this militarised area, part of the 31,760 acres of Dartmoor currently leased or owned by the Ministry of Defence as the Dartmoor Training Area. The permanent camp was started in 1892, although there had been a temporary camp near there since 1875 where the army, particularly the artillery, did their Autumn Manoeuvres. The recorded army presence on Dartmoor goes at least as far back as 1809 when the army were operating as guards over the Napoleonic and American war prisoners at Princetown jail.

In the same way that the remoteness and emptiness of this land made it a good place to isolate captives, it was the shape and character of the terrain that attracted the army here. The stone tors with their ankle-breaking clitter, the steep hills and quick mountain rivers, and the boggy ground were welcomed as a stand-in for the high lands of Europe and the rest of the world. In this way, people, largely from outside of the moor, added extra layers to the idea of Dartmoor's grimness. It was already thought to be a barren waste where nothing could grow, and establishing facilities for dealing in human misery and death only enhanced this perception.

Rock basin from the side

Rowtor stack

The soldiers stationed here certainly felt the landscape was an enemy, or the next best thing. An American soldier at the camp in the run-up to the Second World War wrote: ' It seemed as though Okehampton must be on the top of England. When the wind blew there, as it did continually, it felt as though there was nothing between us and the North Pole but a wire fence, the gate of which had been left open. It rained often on the moors, and then the country took on an even more bleak and desolate appearance. One thing we could be sure of: it was good training for combat, for if a man could come through these spells on the moors, nothing nature could devise could have any effect on his health or morale.'

As we hiked up towards Rowtor, on our route to West Mill Tor, we came across another good example of our tendency to project ourselves onto the land. We had spotted some incongruous-looking dots of red nestling underfoot. This is a lichen called *Cladonia floerkeana*, which is mostly a delicate pale green but has hollow branches with lurid scarlet tips. This has earned it the common name of British Soldier Lichen, the khaki bodies and red tips reminiscent of the red caps of the Royal Military Police.

Nowadays there is more concern for the moor as a friend, with the army cooperating with other agencies to ensure that the environmental impact of training exercises is low. The moor still bears many scars though, and every year walkers come across some of the tonnes of ordnance that is still buried on the moor which is sometimes very dangerous. In 1995 three children letterboxing near Great Mis Tor were injured when they found a shell from army exercises in 1943 that exploded.

As we reached the summit of Rowtor the granite shapes came alive and we noticed a tall, isolated stack, capped with an enormous lintel leaning precariously over a large empty space. Below the lintel was a tall thin crevice into which it was possible to climb. Inside the void, it felt dark, cold, quiet and damp. It was a strange feeling of protection, like being inside a living being – albeit a cold, still one.

Emerging from this mineral shelter to crackling sounds, we heard gunshots peppering the air and saw a dark green military truck grinding along the track between us and West Mill Tor. Although we'd checked the firing times and there was no live firing, exercises were underway. We watched as the truck came to a halt and disgorged four squaddies who fanned out and covered all directions. At some unseen signal, they started running towards what looked like a grass-covered stone igloo, before scaling a large bank to its side and disappearing off into the distance.

This odd feature is a fascinating military remnant, the remains of an old target railway which was used right up until the 1960s. The idea was that troops could practise firing at a moving target, which ran on a trolley along the metal tracks, which are still in situ. Whether for practical or sentimental reasons, the small locomotive which pulled the target is still inside the shed (the igloo-shaped building which is usually locked).

As we yomped down the other side of Rowtor we heard the deep thumping sound of a military helicopter, shortly followed by its dark silhouette flying past, with three large bags of rocks dangling below. Following the stones in flight as they swung past the tor we started climbing up the clitter-strewn slopes, exploded outwards by thousands of years of erosion. The sheer volume of it on this hillside suggests that West Mill tor was massive at one point. We could see a very fine cliff on its southern side, and numerous individual outlying outcrops around it, like sentinel posts.

At the most northerly stack we found the clearing and the 'wing wall' as described by Eric Hemery. It had an unusual side with a cuboid feel; the granite was formed in a grid of squares like a giant game of noughts and crosses. Standing on top of the wall, we surprised a soldier sitting below having a cigarette, the rest of his patrol established around the perimeter of the tor. They ignored us, used to being interrupted by gore-tex-clad civilians, as we headed south towards the biggest and most dramatic part of the tor. Coming at it from the western side, we looked up and noticed some serpentine depressions above us in the side of the top of one of the pillars, calling to mind the curves of a Henry Moore mother and child sculpture. A short climb later, with some slightly hairy balancing on the top rock, we found three large rock basins, bowls with notches on the side, where water and ice had carved an overflow, draining down the tor face. On the eastern edge there was another stack with about 10 smaller basins on its summit.

We walked around to the southernmost flank of the tor which had a lot of vertical as well as horizontal jointing, making it look cross-hatched. Leaning out over the edge was a formation of rocks with a large overhang which looked just like Mr Punch in profile. We sat below it eating our lunch, watching purple smoke rising in a plume in the distance as soldiers hidden in the valley of Black a Ven Brook carried out their exercises.

British Soldier Lichen

Fortified by our rations, we headed south towards the purple smoke to visit East Mill Tor. The soldiers seemed to have moved off by the time we reached the brook at New Bridge, but we found more on sentry duty on the top of the tor, defending this shattered granite outpost. As they scanned the moor with binoculars for enemies camouflaged in the endless grasses, we looked south towards Princetown. How different this part of the moor looks from the rest of Dartmoor. There is an epic, bright smoothness to it. Great shoulders of hillside, devoid of trees, spread into the distance, giving the tors a particular drama as they guard the rolling moor and rushing sky.

INFORMATION

WEST MILL TOR:
50.7011, -4.0015, SX 58752 90965, What3Words: tomato.defenders.headline

ALSO OF INTEREST:
Old target railway: 50.7023, -3.9942, SX 59289 91105, What3Words: handsets.expand.units
Rock basins at the southern tip of West Mil Tor: 50.7008, -4.0014, SX 58756 90934, What3Words: grunt.loaning.concerts
Rowtor: 50.7074, -3.9937, SX 59321 91652, What3Words: bump.seasick.sharpened
East Mil Tor: 50.6940, -3.9850, SX 59893 90152 What3Words: grub.universe.slipped

ACCESS:
This area is in the Okehampton Firing Range: check firing times before you set out on the Government website: www.gov.uk/government/publications/dartmoor-firing-programme. There is a car park north-east of Rowtor, near Okehampton Camp (what3words: dreams.mainland.difficult). From the car park head south-west over Row Tor and then continue south-west to West Mill Tor. It's a walk of about a mile. You can extend the walk south-east to East Mill Tor from where you can head back north to the car park.

View towards Rowtor from the north

LUCKEY TOR

'Here, close to the stream, is Lug Tor, sometimes called Lucky Tor, and also the Raven Rock. It is a mass of granite draped with ivy, and resembles a ruined castle. Some times it is spoken of as the Eagle Rock.'

William Crossing, *Crossing's Guide to Dartmoor*, 1912

On a late March day, we drove over the moor towards Dartmeet. The weather was turbulent: great grey scudding clouds and pelting rain. The original plan had been to hike up Yar Tor but that felt too exposed so we switched plans and decided to walk south along the Dart Valley to Luckey Tor instead. It started to hail and we braced ourselves for getting soaked.

The walk south from Dartmeet along the bottom of the Dart Gorge is an exhilarating experience at any time of year. It is a cinematic sequence of white rushing water, ancient trees bowing in the wind and the chlorophyll lushness of piles of moss-covered boulders. In the spring and summer, wild flowers abound: yellow primroses and common cow wheat, bluebells, and raspberry ripple honeysuckle everywhere. The river swells and becomes more intense as you get deeper into the gorge, with a deep magic of enchanting cascades, sparkling falls and piskie pools, the water running peaty rich but crystal clear over the granite bedrock. In winter it is wilder, as tonnes of frothing water drain from the granite sponge of growan above into this narrow gutter, forever grinding stone, felling trees, and even sometimes claiming lives. When it is like this we have sometimes come across the pathetic sight of a swollen white fleece and a black snout, jammed between the riverside rocks.

We crossed the bridge and headed downriver. The ground underfoot was absolutely sodden, after weeks of rain, with Dartmoor, according to news reports, having five times the usual amount of rainfall in the last couple of months. Then, in recent days, there'd been snow as well. The river was high, scouring the smooth round stones along its edge that are normally dry. As we got further into the gorge the path kept disappearing and we had to clamber over mossy boulders, climbing up and away from the river, to try and keep our feet dry.

We passed Combestone Island and the sun burst out from behind inky grey clouds. What a transformation. Although the trees weren't yet in leaf, the bright green of the ubiquitous moss glowed in the sunlight. The hillside to our left was covered with granite blocks and twisted trees, each one softened by an astrakhan coat of mosses that love the constant moisture: fringe mosses, hair caps, and feather mosses. Everywhere felt electric green and lush. The trees dripped with rain and sunlight; a real temperate rainforest, the air damp, ferns bursting forth from the branches of the trees.

And yet a hundred years ago there were far fewer trees here. A beautiful drawing by P H Rogers from the 1826 book *Dartmoor: A Descriptive Poem* by N T Carrington (opposite), illustrates this well, and is reproduced here.

Before we could reach the tor, we had a large bog to contend with. The Row Brook is a little stream that comes down from higher up; it was raging and had burst its banks all over the surrounding area. We used boulders as stepping stones to get through the spongy ground, before arriving in the clearing in front of Luckey Tor.

The first sight of this tor, seen from the river approach, is unforgettable. The Row Brook runs directly in front of it, making an effective moat. The tor looms up squarely from the valley floor, dwarfing everything around it, framed in a close-cropped clearing which is a popular place to bivouac. On many a summer's night, the flames of a campfire animate the rock face. Its position feels special. Most tors are at the summit of a hill, dominating the views for miles around, standing grandly in the landscape, devoid of trees. Luckey Tor is sequestered in the folds of the Dart Valley, and in the summer mostly obscured by foliage; when you find it you feel as though you've discovered a secret kingdom.

There is also a hidden swimming spot in front of Luckey Tor called Black Pool, which like the tor, is concealed and easy to miss, as there is a small island in front of it. It is bounded by a sheer cliff on the opposite bank, which creates a waterfall's veil to the right. On a summer's evening, the setting sun shines from the west straight onto the pool's black depths.

On the Ordnance Survey map, the rock is called Luckey Tor, but it has had various names over the years. Eric Hemery, in *High Dartmoor*, calls it Looka Tor, arguing that 'this lofty riverside bastion…was a natural watch-tower for the confederates of those who were poaching, smuggling or sheep-rustling under the concealment of the heavily wooded sides of the gorge; that it was, in fact, a look-out tor, as was, though for less clandestine purposes.' The rock is also very popular with climbers, who have their own route nomenclature. They have given the different parts of the tor, and the routes, various names, making a poetry of its parts: Ivy Wall, the Eyrie, Eagle's Nest, The Grockel, Windy Ceiling, Bloodshot, Black Jam Crack…

We gazed up at it, Sleeping Beauty's castle, shrouded by trees. We wandered around the front of it, admiring its southern face which was angular and faceted. From the western side, it reared up dramatically, and from the east, we imagined a craggy face in the giant blocks, perhaps (fairy tale

Luckey Tor summit

Endangered Oil Beetle

mash-up) Sleeping Beauty's Beast? We walked around the left-hand side and started to climb up to the top where we found a long and low cave just below the summit, shaped like a sleeping compartment or couchette in a train. It looked like the perfect place for Beauty to spend the night, tucked up in her bivvy bag; sheltered from the storm. Then we spotted a candle stump on an internal rock, and the remains of a fire; it seemed she had already been.

The top of the tor was long and flat; we found another unusual rectangular hollow space that had the feel of a coffin or kistvaen. We stood on the precipice looking south over the wooded hillside on the other side, where there is a clearing by the river. We thought back to the summer of the pandemic, in 2020, when a group called the Rainbow Family of Living Light set up camp there. About a hundred people camped illegally by the river, with the police responding by setting up a road block on the only nearby road, infuriating locals and visitors who couldn't access the moor. The authorities, including the police and Dartmoor National Park, seemed powerless to do anything else and so for a few weeks this deserted spot became a counter-cultural fairy story, a mini-Woodstock, with naked yoga and skinny dipping, camp-fire story-telling and dream-catcher making.

We turned away from the precipice, heading north along the top of the tor, and then left the rocks to walk uphill alongside the Row Brook, admiring its many small waterfalls. A handy fallen tree made a perfect bridge, and we crossed over and followed the stone wall of Rowbrook Farm, until we were back under the racing white clouds up on the top of the moor. We passed through the remains of a Bronze Age settlement before heading back down the hill to Dartmeet.

INFORMATION

LUCKEY TOR:
50.5334, -3.8568, SX 68475 72051,
What3Words: durations.general.rank
ALSO OF INTEREST:
The Couchette: 50.5334 , -3.8572, SX 68473 72052, What3Words: montage.animal.galloped
BLACK POOL: 50.5326 , -3.8575, SX 68446 71967, What3words: fidgeting.hint.marble
Bronze age settlement: 50.5379 , -3.8655, SX 67895 72566, What3Words: tolerates.misfits.train
ACCESS:
Luckey Tor is quite tough to get to. It is in a very remote spot, right at the heart of the Dart Gorge. You can either start at the car park at Dartmeet (What3words: angle.swing.blackbird) and then cross the road bridge and walk downstream until you reach Luckey Tor. This involves a lot of boulder and bog hopping, particularly towards the end, and conditions are slippery after wet weather. The other way is to park on the road above Dartmeet (What3Words: selling. regarding.mergers) and hike down from the top of the moor, which also involves a bit of clambering as you near the tor, and crossing the Row Brook stream.

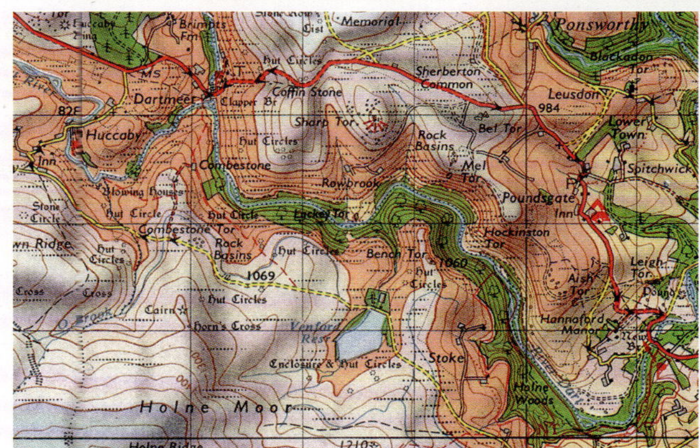

Haircap Moss

'Couchette', Luckey Tor

FOX TOR

'In certain weather conditions the wind moans weirdly through the gaps and fissures of Fox Tor, and the hill presents a veiled, slightly sinister aspect to the distant viewer, on the north rim of the Central Basin. The piping of curlew over the Great Mire rises on the north wind in spring and autumn to Fox Tor: with this in my ears I descended from Black Lane to the tor on a golden evening of early winter in 1978 and watched a huge sun sink low beneath a pall of purple cloud, painting Cramber Down and Chants Hill rose pink.'

Eric Hemery, *High Dartmoor,* 1983

Arriving at Whiteworks on a bright and breezy April afternoon we were struck by the enormity of the landscape before us, strange in its desolation, starkly sublime. Looking across the gigantic broken basin formed by the crests of Ter Hill, Crane Hill and the central Princetown ridge, we could see few features; just miles of ochre brown moorland stretching as far as the eye could see. Alex pointed out a tiny black dot on a faraway hill, 'that's Fox Tor'. It looked both terribly far away and yet reachable with an outstretched hand; in fact it was only 2 miles away. There was something forbidding about the prospect of the walk. The silence and vastness of the moor made us feel as though we were earth-bound lunar explorers entering into the unknown.

For some, the name Fox Tor will inevitably conjure up images of huge bogs and remote wastes: it is forever associated with Fox Tor Mire, which fills the bottom of the basin, and is one of the largest bogs on Dartmoor. It is thought to have been the inspiration for the Great Grimpen Mire in *The Hound of the Baskervilles* by Sir Arthur Conan Doyle, who stayed in nearby Princetown in 1901, where he started writing his famous novel. He no doubt took many walks around the sweating granite walls of the prison and out from the village onto the moor. His mind would have been crowded with thoughts of dark, desperate, escaped convicts and gruesome deaths in bottomless black peat mires. This stony, moorland atmosphere was masterfully evoked by Sidney Paget in his black-and-white illustrations of the tale (see page 58). Also very near Fox Tor is Childe's Tomb, the source of one of Dartmoor's most famous and gruesome legends; so a literary expedition to this part of the moor is undoubtedly eerie.

Gazing at Fox Tor in the distance, it seemed obvious to walk in a straight line towards it. However, as William Crossing advises in his famous guide to Dartmoor: 'A mire is of a totally different character to the fen; it is really a swamp, and is usually found at the heads of streams. Should the rambler walk into one, he must at once retrace his steps, and on no account attempt to go forward.'

So, although, looking at the map, we could see a bridle path leading south from Whiteworks

Sidney Paget illustration from *Hound of the Baskervilles*

Childe's Tomb

heading towards Fox Tor, we didn't take it. This is one of those ghost routes that occasionally appear on the map: there isn't actually a passable path for mere mortals. Instead, we set off south, along Devonport Leat. This man-made watercourse was built between 1795 and 1802 to supply water to the docks at Plymouth and still flows well today. It takes water from the Blackabrook, West Dart and Cowsic rivers and runs for over 40 miles across Dartmoor and down to Devonport.

As we followed the leat, we admired its clear waters flowing over green weed and gurgling brightly, and reflected on the workers who built it over two hundred years ago. Where did they come from and where did they stay? Did they have to camp while carrying out this back-breaking work in this isolated place? It must have been very hard work digging out the channel, and then building the walls out of granite. We noticed what looked like a clapper bridge over the leat, stones protruding over the water, but with the middle stone missing. We assumed it was broken, but later learnt it was a 'sheep leap' to enable sheep to cross. With all these interventions on the moor throughout history there is always plenty to puzzle out on the ground.

Turning away from the leat, we followed a long stone newtake wall east towards Fox Tor. The wall grew more substantial, the further we walked, and we realised it was similar to a ha ha, with a sunken ditch on the other side. Wooden ladders were placed at intervals along the wall; one bearing a sign saying it had been put there by the Dartmoor National Park Ranger Service, assisted by volunteers, but not giving a date. Judging by the amount of lichen on the ladders, and the fragile state of some of them, it was some time ago.

Fox Tor, in the distance, started to get bigger,

and we left the wall to climb up the hill towards it. We saw that the landscape, which had seemed so monotonous, viewed from the car, was remarkably diverse and full of grasses including bristle bent, common bent, sheep's fescue, and purple moor grass. We passed a series of large round holes in the ground, as well as gullies and spoil heaps; remnants of the tin mining that went on here for centuries. Once on the ridge, Fox Tor seemed further away than ever; the way things appear in such open terrain changes all the time; it felt as though were inside a mirage.

Finally, we arrived at the tor where the first thing we noticed was a huge rock that looked like a massive horse's hoof. This was on the north-western pile. Feeling tired, we sat down out of the wind behind one of the stacks and had a cup of tea and some rich Highland shortie biscuits.

Revived, we set off to explore and found three distinct stacks. We were especially keen to find an unusual feature on the southern pile we'd read about in *High Dartmoor* by Eric Hemery. He describes '...an object of great interest in the fallen summit-rock that bears on its surface two large basins like eye-sockets in the skull of a mammoth greater than pre-history ever knew. The

larger of these hollows has a diameter of three feet. From the angle of each may be deduced the two successive and perilous positions of the rock on the summit of the tor at least thirteen thousand years ago, weathering having first tilted it to form a second basin and then released it to crash to the ground.'

As we approached the southern stack, the sun shone brightly through holes in the rock, and we noticed a rectangular cavity right at the bottom, the shape and size of a letterbox, presumably man-made. We made our way around the pile and found, to our great excitement, Hemery's 'mammoth skull'. This was the first time we had ever seen rock basins on their side like this. The two great hollows, like eyes, were very striking, although instead of seeing a mammoth, Sophie's subconscious instead threw up an image of Donald Duck.

Next, we headed north for a short distance to find Childe's Tomb. (Seen here in an engraving by P H Rogers from *Dartmoor: A Descriptive Poem* by NT Carrington 1826). According to legend, Childe, a medieval squire from near Plymouth, got stuck in a raging blizzard while out riding on the moor. To try to stay alive, he killed his horse and disembowelled it so he could climb inside its body to stay warm. Sadly, he failed and froze to death, leaving a note declaring whoever found his body and ensured a Christian burial, would inherit his land. A macabre race then took place between the abbeys of Tavistock and Buckfast to be the first to recover the body.

We reached the tomb and found a stone cross sitting on several large blocks of granite surrounded by a ring of huge kerb stones. It's not known how old the cross is, or who put it there originally. But it is highly likely that it was placed on top of a prehistoric burial place, probably a stone kist. We stopped and sat there for a while. Looking out over the mire, a sense of isolation crept over us. This would have been a miserable place to die as the storm took hold, the smell of entrails filling the nostrils and the swirling whiteness in the black dark gradually swallowing up the eyes and mind. We hurried back to the wall, and did a loop around Nun's Cross Farm, grim, shuttered, and flanked by two dark pine trees, before heading back to the comforting warmth of the car.

INFORMATION

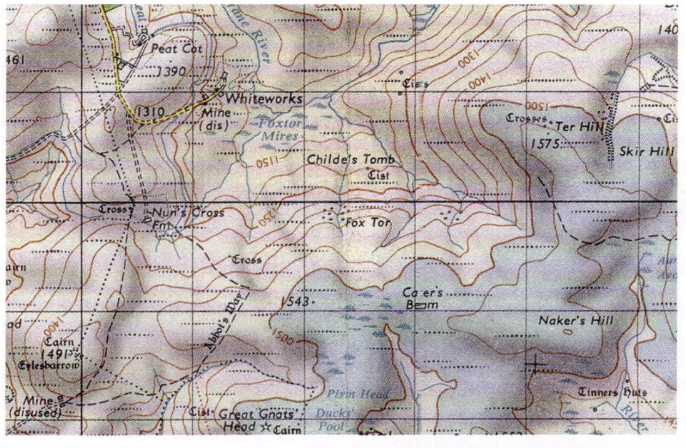

FOX TOR:
50.5119, -3.9391, SX 62603 69817, What3Words: spun.overused.jeep

ALSO OF INTEREST:
Mammoth's Skull: 50.5117, -3.9390, SX 62614 69789, What3Words: intro.hats.compress
Childe's Tomb: 50.5162, -3.9397, SX 62573 70294, What3Words: used.bulldozer.qualified
Nun's Cross Farm: 50.5115, -3.9677, SX 60579 69824, What3Words: materials.sympathy.drilled

ACCESS:
There are a couple of pull-ins by the road near Whiteworks: the best is by a bridge (What3words: readjust.unto.heats); there is another a little further west (What3Words: demanding.helm.bolt). The safest way to reach the tor is to walk along the man-made elements in the area. Start by walking south along Devonport Leat; after about two-thirds of a mile, the route heads east along a stone wall that crosses numerous tiny streams (you can cross them by walking along the wall itself which incorporates stone bridges). When you can see Fox Tor off to the right, it is safe to head off away from the wall, walking uphill towards the tor in the distance. From the tor, you can walk directly north for a short distance to reach Childe's Tomb.

Mammoth's skull

Nun's Cross Farm

GREAT MIS TOR

'Pursuing your way upwards, climb to the top of Great Mis Tor, though the hill is long. Druidical origin has been claimed for the great rock basin on the top, which is very perfect and even appears to have a channel for letting off the water. The moormen, however, will tell you that Mis Tor Pan is sometimes called the Devil's Frying Pan.'

Beatrix F Cresswell and P H W Almy, *The Homeland Guide to Dartmoor*, 1948

Unlike most tors, Great Mis Tor has been mentioned in the literature of Dartmoor for nearly eight centuries, under various names including Mistor and Mistor Pan. As far as we know it was first mentioned in the 1240 Perambulation of Dartmoor as Mystor, as part of the boundary of Dartmoor Forest that was walked by twelve knights under the order of King Henry III, to confirm the extent of his lands.

It is one of the most magnificent tors on Dartmoor, mainly because of its position. Although it is not as tall as some of those around it, the views from the top are extensive. Standing on the top, looking south, you can almost hear the breakers of the sea down at Plymouth Sound, and the lapping of the River Tamar which you can see snaking up the valley. In the foreground, the renowned Merrivale ceremonial stone rows are visible. Turning west, you see a magnificent trio of tors, like a miniature mountain range, and the tiny River Walkham, running down below. In the same direction, if you look carefully, you can see the Langstone Moor stone circle, as well as the ancient church of St Michael de Rupe capping the volcanic plug of Brent Tor in the far distance. Turning north, the vast grasslands of the northern plain of the moor stretch out before you, a huge contrast to the man-made environments to the south and the busy city and docks of Plymouth. Altogether, Great Mis Tor is an awe-inspiring place.

We went to visit it on May Day. It felt distinctly unsummery as we started to hike up the military track which leads gradually uphill to the tor. Slate grey clouds hung over us, accompanied by an icy wind from the east, only occasionally punctuated by the odd ray of sun. The larks though, appeared to have got the summer memo: they were singing constantly overhead. We were excited to explore Great Mis Tor because we'd read about some unusual features on it, in particular, a very large rock basin.

Over to our left, three tors stood grandly on a ridge: Middle Staple Tor, Great Staple Tor and Roos Tor, the boggy troughs between them dipping like swags in a baronial drawing room. Up ahead we could see our target of Great Mis Tor, a citadel on the summit topped with a flag. In front of it, nearer us, but still some distance away, stood Little Mis Tor, an outlying fortification with three distinct turrets, defending the great tor behind it. But as we grew nearer, the turrets seemed

to dissolve and it became less distinctive, like one big piece of rock. The old name for it, Wain Tor, seems to reflect this; close up, it looked like an old-fashioned cart. We climbed up its main pile and found a couple of small rock basins on the eastern side. A smaller outcrop, a rectangular cuboid with unusually straight sides, stood nearby, like its driver.

We carried on uphill through increasing amounts of clitter until we reached Great Mis Tor. The red flag was flying from the mast on the highest part, indicating army manoeuvres in the Merrivale range close by; we could hear gunshots over to the east. We were struck by the sheer extent of the tor. It spread all over the summit of the hill, with several large, long outcrops running roughly north-south. We walked around the largest, where the flagpole stood. There was a huge, very flat cliff on its western side, with prominent horizontal grooves, and a rock tower protruded, right next to the flagpole.

The rocks were very varied: as well as the more pointed forms, many more fluid, bulbous shapes seemed to drip and melt at strange organic angles. This impression was enhanced in places by the undulating lichens clinging to them, large black spots on the vertical rock surfaces, dark holes made glistening wet by the constant water oozing from a spring inside the tor, making it an uncanny sight. It reminded us why many lichens are named after injuries: *Lecidella stigmatea* for the stigmata, the bleeding holes made in the hands and feet of Jesus Christ at the crucifixion; *Haematomma coccineum* the bloodspot lichen; *Leptonium lacerum* the wound lichen; and *Porpida tuberculosa* named after diseased human skin.

The tor's most famous feature is a very large rock basin on the main outcrop near where the flag flies. These basins, which are usually found on the tops of tors, have been the subject of speculation over the years, particularly about them being created by Druids for sacrificial rites. However, the consensus now is that they are natural, created by weathering. As William Crossing counters in his famous guide to Dartmoor, 'the battle has been fought, and the geologists have won; these basins are now fully recognised as of natural formation.' However, just because they are naturally formed does not mean they were not seen as a remarkable feature by our ancestors who lived here, who would have noticed anything unusual like this immediately. So perhaps they were still chosen for ritual, as the Victorian writers suggested. Certainly some contemporary pagans are still inspired by them today, offering oak and holly to the waters in this font of living rock.

We clambered up the northern end of the main outcrop and walked south along the top of it to find the rock basin. It was a large, round and elegant circular hollow, wet and dark, with a channel on one side with water dripping out. We were disappointed not to see it filled with dark blood as our imaginations had made it so (but also really pleased it wasn't).

The Devil's Frying Pan

As we climbed down, we saw a handsome wheatear hopping off one of the outcrops. These birds are summer visitors and are often seen on Dartmoor where they usually stay close to the ground. The name comes from the old Saxon English for white (wheat) and arse (ear) referring to their white rump, a name too rude for some. It continued to flutter around as we carried on exploring.

We were also keen to find a couple of other features that we'd read about. The first was an unusual rock we'd seen in *Worth's Dartmoor* (1953). A photograph in the book (opposite) shows an unusual rocky mass, described as being on Great Mis Tor, which he refers to as a 'rounded block', teetering precariously on top of another one, rather like a logan stone. The same rock is also pictured, looking rather like an hourglass, in a beautiful drawing (opposite) in an 1885 book called *English Pictures*, by Samuel Manning and S G Green, although described as being at Little Mis Tor (which is very nearby). It also gets a mention in an 1836 book by Anna Eliza Bray, *The Borders of the Tamar and the Tavy*, who talks about '...a singularly formed rock; from its appearance, we concluded it was a logan-stone, but tried in vain to move it.'

We searched in vain for this rock, but could not find anything resembling it. Concluding it must have fallen, we tried to find its remains. There were possible locations, but it was impossible for us to be sure; it reappeared in our imagination everywhere. Presumably, this airy edifice is lying smashed and unrecognisable, claimed by the inexorable force of gravity in the past 100 years.

The other feature we wanted to find was a 'chasm amid the rocks' which was mentioned by Anna Eliza Bray as a place where she and her party sheltered from a shower of rain, and 'made them echo with the voice of song'. Eric Hemery in *High Dartmoor* (1983) also talks about going into the chasm with his son. We hunted around for this echoing fissure where you could shelter from the weather, until on the western side of the hill, at the southern end of another long outcrop, we found what looked like a large gateway framing a tall recess in the rock, overhung by a five-fingered granite canopy that looked like a huge hand resting on a grand columned doorway. There was a piece of smooth stone on the ground like a doormat and even a handy flat stone to the side that made a suitably grand throne. However, the recess was very shallow and we couldn't get 'inside' the rock very far, was it really the mysterious 'chasm'? It was certainly the closest thing we could find to it.

Having circled the tor, we headed down to the pretty river Walkham, to a small weir that feeds the Merrivale granite quarry leat. Turning south, we passed through the remains of a Bronze Age village with several quite distinct hut circles camouflaged in great fields of broken stone. These large quantities of stone are known locally as clitter or clatter, the same words used to describe a rattling sound, like the sound of rocks shaken together. The rocks were silent today, although we did hear an echo of their once noisy descent down this slope in the distant crackle of gunfire from the army exercises.

Postscript It was only, several months later, re-examining the photos, we realised we had found the rock mentioned by Worth and Anna Eliza Bray, and depicted in *English Pictures*., but hadn't realised it at the time. We had inadvertently taken a picture of it when exploring the tor, and it was only by looking at the image again, in comparison with Worth's picture, that we realised it was one and the same, but, as we thought, had fallen off.

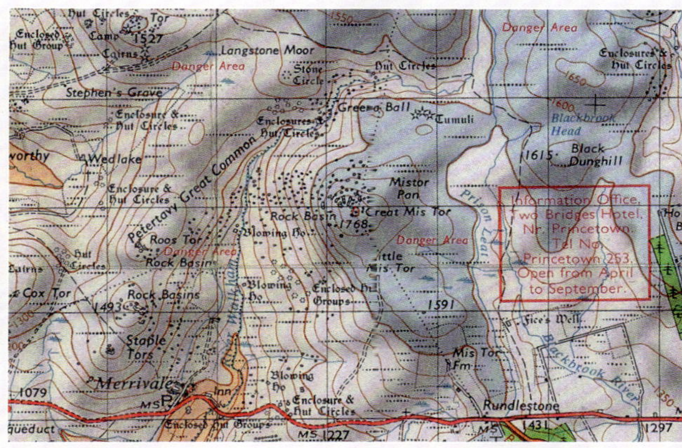

GREAT MIS TOR:

50.5741, -4.0309, SX 56285 76905, What3Words: calls.totals.hiker

ALSO OF INTEREST:

Large rock basin on the main outcrop (with the flagpole): 50.5743, -4.0312, SX 56262 76931 What3Words: indicate.transcribes.taxed.

Large 'doorway' overhung by a rocky 'hand': 50.5747, -4.0329, SX 56150 76974, What3Words: sandpaper.grants.cemented

ACCESS:

Park at Four Winds car park (What3Words: romantics.spins.masters). From here cross the road and walk north along the track which takes you straight up to Great Mis Tor. You can then do an anticlockwise circle back to the car, by heading west and then following the River Walkham south for a while, before heading south-west through the Bronze Age village and back to the car park.

Could this be the 'rounded block' mentioned by Worth and featured in *English Pictures?*

LITTLE MIS TOR.

'Rounded Block' pictured in *Worth's Dartmoor*

UGBOROUGH BEACON

'…the Eastern Beacon …forms a conspicuous object on the southern borders of the moor, and is crowned with a characteristic tor, the western pile of which is surrounded by a cairn-like agglomeration of stones. We shall observe that all the neighbouring heights are crowned with cairns… Of all the views gained from the border-heights of Dartmoor, none is more extensive, varied, and interesting, than that which greets the eye from this the southernmost point of the great Devonshire moorlands.'

Samuel Rowe, *A Perambulation of the Antient and Royal Forest of Dartmoor,* 1856

Ugborough Beacon stands in solitude, the only tor on this flank of the moor. This southern expanse of Dartmoor is notable for the absence of tors, but what it has instead, in abundance, are cairns, great piles of stones which mark ancient burial places. They sit atop the highest points to the north, west and south of the beacon; as you stand on the tor looking across to these huge mounds of stones, you have a sense of being somewhere truly inhabited by our ancestors, where they marked the land with the stones as part of their rituals, and the land marked them.

Another unusual thing about Ugborough Beacon is that it incorporates a cairn – about 25 metres wide and about 1.5 metres high - which has been created around an outcrop on its western side. These constructions are known as tor cairns. There are others on Dartmoor, for example at Rippon Tor, Corndon Tor and White Tor, where Neolithic peoples worked with the natural rock eminences to lend height and mass to their monuments. There is no doubt that the height of the land was significant in the choice of these memorials and ritual sites, and that tors were at the apex of these high places. The vista of skies, the sun, the moon and the stars from here must have been, for our ancestors, part of a mystical other world for the living and the dead.

The Beacon occupies a commanding position high on the edge of the moor, overlooking the lowlands below. Views from here are far-reaching. Not just over to the cairns which adorn the skyline mainly to the west, but south, down to the South Hams and out to sea. On top of this tor, you truly feel in touch with all you survey. Given its position and name, it is not surprising that in the past fires were lit here, to announce news or to celebrate events. Written records from the seventeenth century support this, but in recent times, such as the Queen's Platinum Jubilee in 2022, the tor has remained dark.

The church clock was striking four as we drove into the dark of a pre-dawn May morning. We wanted to see the tor at sunrise, given its ideal position on the eastern side of the moor facing the new day, but the 'getting up at 3:30 am' part of the equation was not such fun. Nevertheless, we were rewarded by the sight of a waxing golden moon, low in the sky, as we drove down the dual carriage-

Tor cairn

Sunrise over Brent Hill

way towards South Brent. Behind us, the sky was already growing lighter.

We drove up the lanes in the gloom, trying to avoid the potholes, and parked at Peek Moor Gate. A tawny owl was hooting, and a buzzard mewing as we started the steep tramp up towards the tor in the dimpsy light; the sun was somewhere behind us. It was hard going but we used every rest stop to turn around and check the sunrise; the sky was changing all the time.

Rather perfectly, the sun was coming up behind the triangle of Brent Hill in the distance. The peachy horizon was turning pink, a shocking pink, and becoming pinker every time we checked, although it was tempered by large granite clouds which hung low and heavy in the sky. As we passed a spindly hawthorn tree, its twisted silhouette black against the dawn, we heard a cuckoo calling from the valley below. Our gaze was drawn to the cairns on the hillside above. In Celtic mythology the cuckoo, appearing when spring leaves winter behind, is a messenger between the living and the dead, the world of dark and the world of light.

We reached the summit and sat down on the tor to watch the sun emerge. The sky got more intense and soon a seraphic glow of rose, gold and orange was spreading more widely, lighting the clouds from beneath. The rocks of the tor were bathed in a warm radiance, and gradually the horizon changed from pink to yellow until the sunlight finally erupted and the exotic colours melted away. It was a magical, fleeting, moment, where we felt a sense of timeless impermanence, a dissolution of our very selves.

Getting up to explore, we found several 10,000-year-old rock basins on the top of the main outcrop on the eastern side, the small pools of water beautifully coruscating in the dawn light. We walked across a small plateau to the western side where we found the cairn: hundreds of stones placed around the small outcrop of tor in the middle. The tor was obviously chosen as a place of significance by the people who created the cairn, but why incorporate it into the monument?

Most cairns are thought to mark a place of the dead, containing a burial chamber or kist for a body, a beaker containing ashes or something similar, long since decayed. It would surely be difficult though to inter a dead person's ashes or bones if building onto rock rather than earth? Maybe ashes were scattered across the bare surface of the stone, the tor itself a partner in death. There was also the possibility that it was the tor itself that was being marked out, the living stone being important as something spiritual, perhaps as a conduit or vehicle to carry the dead to the next world. Perhaps being joined to the natural rock gave these memorials more time, the permanence of the stone rooted far into the earth at their core, allowing the memories set down to last longer and be projected further into the future. We thought about the deep time of the tor, the time of people who lived here before us, many thousands of years before us, and we reflected on our own mortality.

We stood by the cairn and looked out towards the sea. Then turning around, we counted six other cairns on the hilltops around us including the Eastern White Barrow – 'the Submarine' –so called because someone in recent times has re-arranged the cairn stones into the round turret of an emergency shelter for stranded walkers, so it looks like an underwater battleship left high and dry on a mountainside. It was a beautiful moment: just us, alone, in this expansive, compelling landscape, the reward for rising before the sun.

From the Beacon, we struck out north-west to seek out the ceremonial elements of this upland necropolis: various megalithic stone rows. We were also hoping to find a ruined chambered tomb, thought to be the only one on Dartmoor. The Rev Hugh Breton, in his book *The Forest of Dartmoor* (1931) called it the 'Coryndon Cromlech'.

Weather, time and people will destroy all things in the end and the first stone row, just west of Spurrell's Cross, was barely visible. The stones were very small and mostly buried. Many megalithic structures were, in fact, minilithic at the outset, and on Dartmoor, the peat has risen around them over thousands of years. They were were raised up with care, only to be robbed for walls or left to go feral. We continued north-east, past another abject row full of lithic pathos, before finding a more substantial example, which was a megalithic anomaly, starting as a single row and then turning into a double row as it continued to flow as a wave downhill towards the West Glaze Brook below.

At Glasscombe Corner, an idyllic spot with a dense clump of beech trees, we sat and had cheese sandwiches for breakfast and listened to crows squabbling over nesting material in the trees above. Further on, to the north-east, there was an unusual set of multiple stone rows; again a highly unusual design for Dartmoor. In *High Dartmoor* (1983) Eric Hemery describes the site as an 'extraordinary complex of stone rows comprising two triple rows, one double and a single - all in parallel '(his italics). It was a cacophony of small stones, they were all around us, some hidden, some visible, and it was hard to discern a pattern.

A short distance away, by Ball Gate (a grand and incongruous gothic monstrosity of dressed stone gate posts with ball finials on top) we found the remains of the 'Coryndon Cromlech'. When originally built, it consisted of three granite uprights a couple of metres high and a capstone weighing many tonnes. It would have been an overwhelming statement of power in this world and the next. Now though, it is laid low by the forces of nature and is just a group of sizeable stones, although you can tell that the largest, which is slightly apart from the rest, was the capstone. It is next to the remains of a barrow of which the dolmen would have formed an entrance, a physical or symbolic focus for celebrating, lighting fires and feasting on pig, ox or lamb.

We retraced our steps to Glasscombe Corner and then followed the West Glaze Brook back to the starting point. Picking our way downhill we were surprised to see a sweet little white and black furry face looking out of a hole in the turf. It was an inexperienced spring lamb that had become trapped underground in a hollow between some stones. As it was muddy, damp and distressed, and unable to get out, we called the Livestock Protection Officer to report it. She told us to grab it by the horns and pull it out. Released from its earthy tomb it fled, mewling, in search of mother. We carried on walking, bolstered by our good deed for the day. If we hadn't happened to pass by, who knows how long the lamb would have been trapped, and whether it would have survived.

The final highlight of the walk was an enchanting waterfall and pool just below Glaze Meet, where the eastern and western branches of the river meet. Crossing famously wrote: 'This is the Wishing Pool, and it is said that those who leap across it, and while doing so loudly express a wish, will obtain what they desire.' Normally we would have swum here, but by this time we were looking forward to getting home and, too tired to leap, were happy just to sit by it for a moment without wanting anything.

INFORMATION

UGBOROUGH BEACON:
50.4169, -3.875, SX 66828 59138, What3Words: button.clipped.cakewalk

ALSO OF INTEREST:
Tor cairn around the western outcrop: 50.4166, -3.8769, SX 66750 59105, What3Words: handle.rank.liberated

Multiple stone rows north-east of Glasscombe Corner: 50.4352, -3.8799, SX 66588 61182, What3Words: glove.presumes.same

Chambered Tomb: 50.4363, -3.8748, SX 66952 61293 What3Words: apparatus.riper.guardian

'Wishing Pool' on the Glaze Brook: 50.4273, -3.8763, SX 66822 60295, What3Words: mailbox.showcase.gracing

ACCESS:
Park at Peek Moor Gate but note there are only a couple of spaces (What3Words: mats.grumble.spurted). Walk north along the field boundary before picking up the footpath to the left which leads uphill to Ugborough Beacon; a walk of about 20 minutes. An alternative place to park is Wrangaton Gate (What3Words: pockets.shades.sway); from here walk along the track north-west, and then north up to Ugborough Beacon.

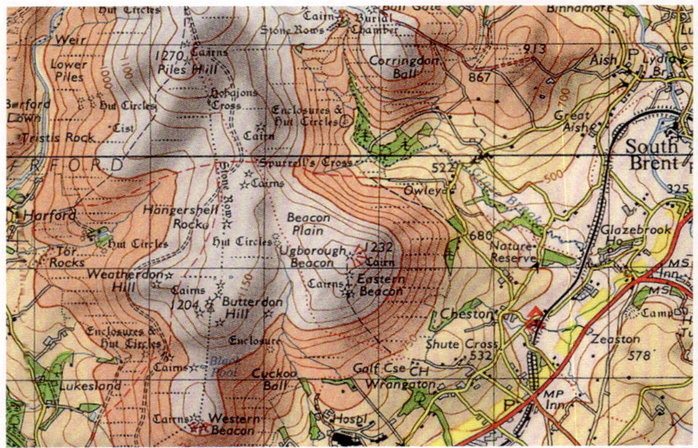

Spurrells Cross

Glasscombe cairn circle

The Wishing Pool

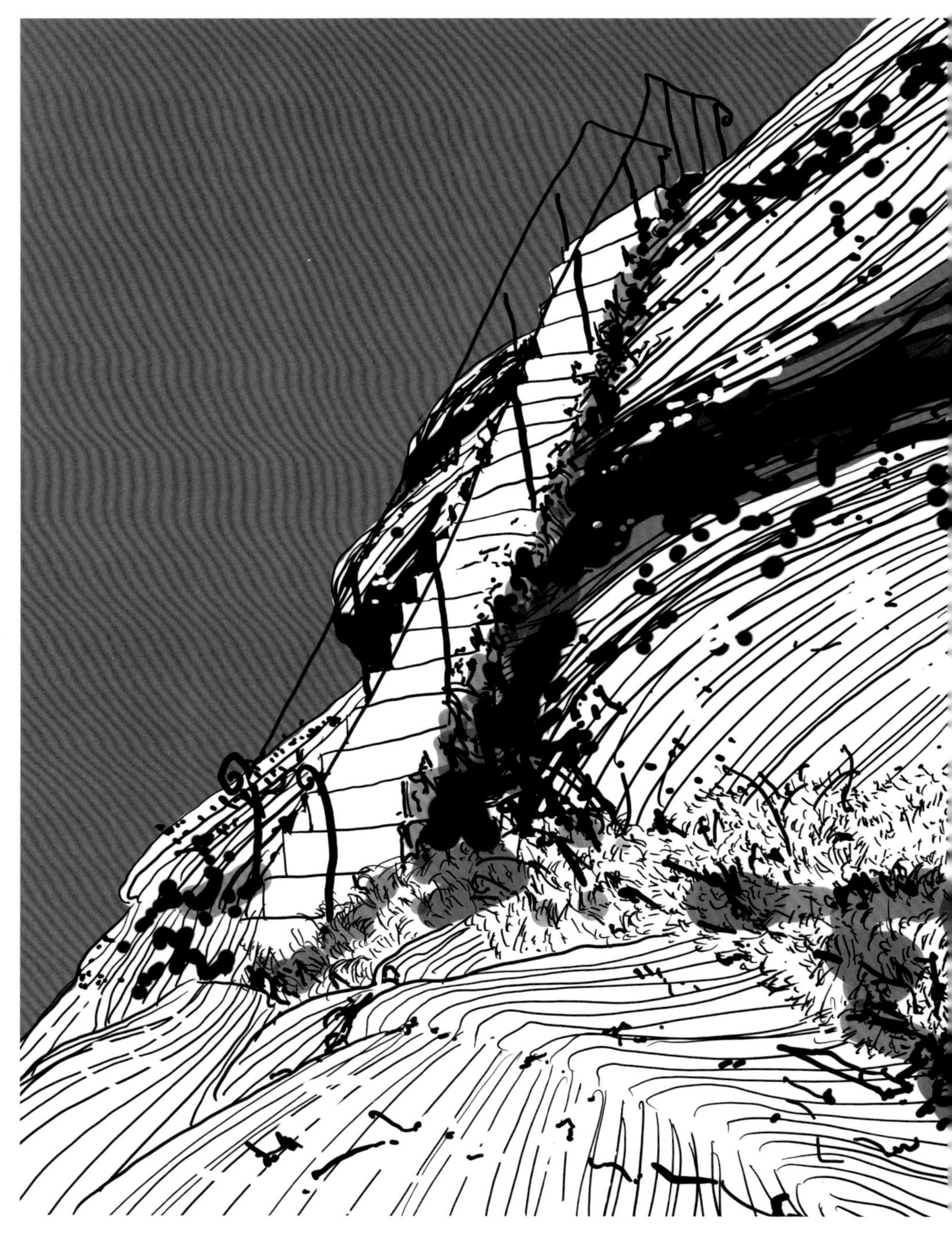

BLACKINGSTONE ROCK

'Leaving Blackystone by the road which winds around its base, we shall proceed somewhat to the north, and, at about the distance of a mile, shall reach Heltor, which occupies an even more commanding position than even Blackystone, as the hill on which it stands rises abruptly from the Vale of the Teign...Viewed from Dunsford it wears the appearance of some antient castle keep, draperied with ivy, and built to defend the pass below…Thus, on the eastern confines of the moor, Heltor and Blackystone are stationed, at the gates of the wilderness…'

Samuel Rowe, *A Perambulation of the Antient and Royal Forest of Dartmoor*, 1856

We call Blackingstone Rock and Heltor the 'twin tors'. They stand in the north-eastern corner of Dartmoor, two great towers marking the border between the moor and the world beyond, the out-land and the in-land as the moor folk call it. Legend, as well as geography, has paired them together. It is said that they are the result of a battle between King Arthur and the Devil who were throwing quoits at each other; their missiles were eventually turned to stone in the form of the two tors. They are also linked in name, as Heltor is also known as White Tor, the yin to Blackingstone's yang.

We set off to visit them on a sultry June afternoon. Their outlying setting makes them unusual: they are surrounded by lush farmland, unlike most tors which are encircled by stark moorscape. The lanes were full of tall, shocking pink foxglove spires and their diminutive mimics, the pale yellow darts of the pennyworts. The whole scene felt burgeoning and green.

The small car park right by Blackingstone Rock – which we will call "Blackystone" as per local tradition – was occupied by a Dartmoor National Park Landrover and another commercial vehicle when we arrived. Fortunately, they left almost immediately, leaving space for us. As we got out of the car we were hit by the sweet smell of summer: honeysuckle and the pungent whiff of bracken. The tor loomed over us and we were immediately seduced by its smooth, flowing form, like melting chocolate. Wild flowers were everywhere, including hawkbit, stitchwort, foxgloves and some gone-over bluebells. There was lots of vegetation growing out of the Blackystone, including rowans, holly and heather. We followed the path around the bottom of it and started climbing up around the side of it, passing under a series of young oak trees in full green leaf.

The sides of the tor fell steeply away above us, like slow-moving lava from a volcano. A tumbling pair of iridescent wood pigeons flew out of a large slit in the rocks above. We got higher and then reached what felt like the back of the rock, which was festooned with soft mosses and peppered with English Stonecrop, a type of sedum with large clumps of pink star-shaped flowers, fed by the

water seeping from the granite's pores. Accompanied by the trill of willow warblers, we turned a corner and came to the most extraordinary feature amid this pastoral glory: a vertiginous stone staircase up one side of the cliff, with elegant, curlicued, wrought-iron hand rails.

This stairway to heaven was constructed in 1870 and is inspected annually for safety by Dartmoor National Park which bought the tor in 1981. It really is a quite remarkable sight, a practical man-made solution for those who wish to enjoy the views from the top of the Blackystone. You really can't imagine the authorities allowing it these days, but luckily for us, the Victorians weren't so worried about health and safety.

The rock was a big attraction in the late 19th century, which may well explain the building of the steps. According to Tim Sandles, author of the *Legendary Dartmoor* website, there were regular charabanc tours that took in the rock and other local beauty spots, often getting stuck in the tiny lanes. He even has a funny story from the Torquay Times of 1890 about the Blackystone being surrounded by turnip fields at the time. Visitors to the rock would scrump these lowly veg, which they would eat on the tor, leaving peelings lying around the place (yes, they did eat them raw).

You need confidence to ascend the staircase as you are climbing steeply up the side of a sheer cliff. The treads are very shallow, and we clung to the handrails with some trepidation. But once at the top – well, it was so worth it. We could see for miles and miles and miles. There were several large rock basins full of water on the top, one of which had three black feathers in it, most likely from a corvid. Perhaps a pair of ravens had been using it as a bird bath. We descended the ladder which was possibly even more scary than climbing it. Safely down, we headed back, enjoying the views of the Blackystone in reverse.

The intention had been to walk the mile or so along the narrow lane to Heltor but laziness got the better of us and we jumped in the car and drove to the permissive path which leads to the rock. As we got out, we glimpsed the elegant form of a young Roe deer, with a chestnut coat, running out of the woods and disappearing quickly down the road. We climbed over the stile and walked along an extremely narrow path, hemmed in by a fence of double barbed wire. We said a silent thank you to whoever had worked to make the tor accessible to all.

We could see the tor rising up in the distance, in a similar fashion to its twin. There was a green and pink vibe as we approached, with clouds of cerise campion, more foxgloves in ranks in the hedge, and more oak trees in full leaf. As we approached, we took in its smooth, melting appearance, but also

Blackystone

noticed something completely different from the Blackystone. It had a strange horizontal seam of pinkish crystalline microgranite which looked exactly like a row of teeth. A lithic impression of the Devil who fought King Arthur perhaps?

We turned a corner to find a deep chasm dividing the tor; it was made up of two separate piles shot through with a profusion of feldspar chips, where we found another line of 'teeth'. There was a large stone at the end of the cleft which made a good place to sit astride, like being on horseback, and take in the views to the west. Next, we climbed up to the top of the northern section. The views from the top were tremendous: the Belvedere at Haldon to the east, the Blackdown Hills behind and the uncountable hills and combes of mid-Devon, culminating in the uplands of Exmoor to the north. We also admired the Blackystone sitting companionably to the south.

Heltor microgranite seam (the 'teeth')

At our feet, we were astonished to find the deepest rock basin we had ever seen – its elephantine curves so deep we could stand in it. There was grass growing in the bottom of it, and also some cigarette ends, charcoal and bottle tops which we cleared up – evidence of the timeless rite of country boys and girls gathering around the fire to drink local cider and make bad choices.

Later, back home, we were doing some research about the tors, and came across a legend about the Blackystone which Sabine Baring-Gould wrote about in the *Book of the West* (1899). He even wrote a ballad about it. It's the sad story of a young mum who also made bad choices and whose baby was eaten by the 'ravens of Blackystone'; all that remained of the child was a 'heap of well-picked bones'. Perhaps the feathers we found in the rock basin at the top of the rock belong to the descendants of those very ravens...

INFORMATION

BLACKINGSTONE ROCK:
50.6573, -3.7182, SX 78640 85590, What3Words: reward.ocean.guidebook
ALSO OF INTEREST:
Heltor: 50.6705, -3.7000, SX 79961 87031, What3Words:debt.shipwreck.boil
ACCESS:
There is a small car park right next to Blackingstone Rock (What3Words: chemistry.twitching.seagull). From here you can walk north up the lane for about a mile to find Heltor. If you'd rather driWve, you can do so and park on the road in a pull-in right next to the footpath up to Heltor (What3Words: keepers.corrode.amuse).

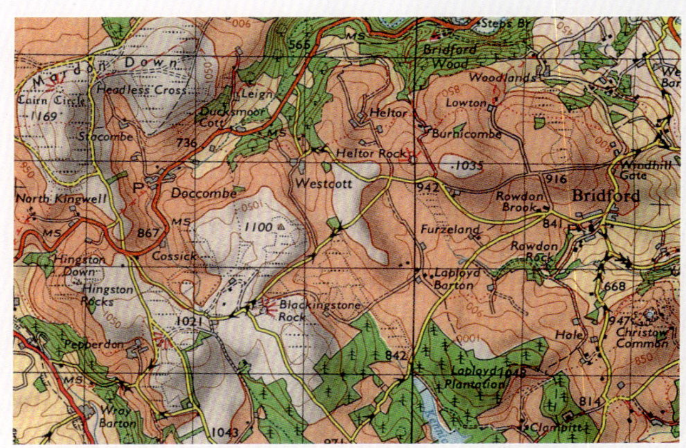

Blackystone rock basins

Stonecrop

DOWN TOR

'The slopes of Down Tor are clittered to a remarkable degree (similar to Vur Tor, Tavy). Numerous huge slabs, lowered upon previous deposits by melting ice are poised in an unconvincing state of balance – their apparent instability discounted by their having occupied such positions for up to thirteen thousand years... The outline of Down Tor is beautiful from any viewpoint and massive on near approach. Visible from the summit are 23 tors and the undulations of countless hills.'

Eric Hemery, *High Dartmoor,* 1983

The summer solstice is a mountain, a peak of light that anticipates a descent into the darker nights that will gradually return, so it felt natural to want to spend it in the high places of Dartmoor, close to the sun. It also felt natural to want to mark this moment in the company of our ancestors on Dartmoor, who, thousands of years ago, corralled the stones of the moor into circles and rows to mark these magical points of the year.

And so we chose Down Tor as the place to visit on the morning of the solstice, June 21st, because it is very near one of the most atmospheric ceremonial sites on Dartmoor. It is a solid peak with far-reaching views to the south over Burrator reservoir and Plymouth Sound, and a panorama taking in Sharpitor, Leather, Sheeps, Gutter, Combeshead and Hen Tors. The tor is worthy of homage in its own right but it also lends its name to one of the most spectacular Bronze Age monuments on the moor: the Down Tor stone row, or, as it is also called, the Hingston Hill stone row. 150 standing stones run in a line almost as far as the eye can see. In front of them is a large cairn circle: a ring of kerb stones surrounding a small barrow which would have contained a stone kistvaen, the final granite tomb of one of the farmers who lived here around 4000 years ago.

Although the body, or its ashes, have long since been reclaimed by the soil, the stones in the row and circle were re-erected at the end of the nineteenth century by members of the Dartmoor Exploration Committee, a group of amateur antiquarians who did a lot of research into the archaeology of the area. Its completeness of design makes it one of the most visually striking ritual sites on Dartmoor, the large stones describing a gentle sideways arc that also ascends the curving hillside.

There is much speculation about the relation these ancient Dartmoor monuments have with the solar system, and whether they were built to mark key moments in the year, notably the solstices and the equinoxes, as has been shown at Stonehenge and elsewhere. There is an interesting book, *Dartmoor Sun*, by Jack Walker, (2005) in which the author visited many of the main prehistoric ritual sites at these times. According to him, on the summer solstice at the Down Tor stone row, the shadows cast by the sun align along the row, delicately connecting each stone with the next. We wanted to visit to see if this was true.

The night before, we checked the forecast and

it looked perfect: a clear morning with no cloud. After a few hours sleep, we followed the cat's eyes across the dark moor roads and, dreamlike, counted the soft white sheep sleeping in groups along the side of the road, their woolly bodies absorbing the stored warmth of the sun held in the tarmac. A tangerine moon hung in an indigo sky over Sharp Tor. Then, to our astonishment, we came across a couple who had managed to drive their car off the road and into a gully, its headlights pointing to the stars. Luckily, they weren't hurt, just stuck, and, using a flashlight, we pointed out a farm 50 yards away, the likely source of a tractor to get them out.

At Princetown, we turned south and the moon was ahead of us, intensified now to a bloody red as it sank into the waters of Plymouth Sound. As we approached Burrator along a deep walled lane, a group of people and a dog appeared in the headlights, walking in the direction of Down Tor, fellow solstice worshippers on their night-time pilgrimage.

It was strangely silent as we walked up the slopes of Down Tor. No birds were singing. Climbing up in the gloaming was a magical experience. We picked our way through a jumble of rocks of different shapes and sizes, and at crazy angles, careful not to take a tumble. In the still twilight, the tor felt arrested in time, a frozen chaos. We pushed on over the top and down the other side in the direction of the row and reached the monument at 4:45, 30 minutes before sunrise was due, hot and sweaty after our yomp in the dimpsy morning light. Someone was already there: a woman with her toy poodle. We chatted about being fellow 'nutters' for getting up so early. More people arrived until in the end we were a group of 11 humans and 3 dogs, standing around waiting for daybreak.

Moonset over Leather Tor

We caught the incense-strong smell of skunk on the breeze and turned round to take in three smoking solstice-worshippers who had arranged themselves on a rock facing the sunrise, donned their shades and were passing round the crisps, all in anticipation of a good show.

Already it was an incredibly dramatic scene. The horizon was saturated with orange, and the stones seemed to float before us. The golden light was warm and gentle, the sky above turning icy blue as the darkness melted. We lit a tea light and placed it in a small cup in the cairn circle, a flame for the dead.

The sun finally appeared at 5:20 as a melting golden dot on the horizon to the west of the stone row. At first, it was not high enough to cast any sunlight on the monument. But gradually, as it got higher, light started to drench the stones, whose shadows pointed at an acute angle to the east of the row. As the sun got higher, we decided to walk to the end of the row; it just called to be walked, processed. At the end was an enormous cairn as well as a large neolithic pound. Standing by the large terminal stone, we made shadow puppets on it with our hands in the sharp sunlight. Walking back, we noticed that the shadows cast by the

Down Tor cairn circle and row

Restoration by the Dartmoor Exploration Committee, 1894 (courtesy Dartmoor Trust)

stones were gradually moving inwards towards the row, as the sun made its way across the heavens.

As clouds of gnats awoke and started to dance amongst the stones, we stood with our backs to the sun, observing the shadows cast by the three large terminal orthostats. We could see that, very gradually, they were moving. We watched, mesmerised, as the shadows aligned, and the largest megalith, like a gnomon on a sundial, cast its shadow right into the centre of the cairn circle: touching that lithic memory of a human life, and the place where our tiny candle was burning. It was a miraculous and moving moment, about an hour after the sun had first shown its head above the horizon. We stayed for a while in this thin place, enraptured. As we watched, the rocks were animated by the rising sun on the longest day of the year, into a living, breathing shrine.

Then it was time to head back to the tor. As we approached from the east, its slopes were now bathed in sunlight, and we could see over to Burrator Reservoir in the distance. As before, we were struck by the eerie shapes of the rocks, many of which seemed to balance precariously; but when we pushed them, they were solid: not a trace of movement. We passed a small tent on the Eastern side of the tor, and the front flap opened and its resident peered out. We didn't have the heart to tell him he'd missed one of the best sunrises ever.

At the top of the tor, we stood on an enormous flat platform of rock, taking in the views. Down Tor has had special meaning for us since the death of our son Felix in 2017. It was one of the last walks we did as a family, and we have a photo of the four of us standing together here, smiling in the weak spring sunshine. It was probably the last image of us all together.

Heading west, we passed a huge cliff festooned with ivy and containing a cave at its foot. Parts of the tor were now bathed in bright sunlight, while others were still in shadow, accentuating its varied shapes. We descended the hill towards the car and found two more outcrops: both unmarked on the map but worthy of note. One had two noticeable narrow columns, and a field wall had been built into it. Someone had left some rosebuds in a niche in the wall, each one individually stuck into the ground.

Solstice sunrise

INFORMATION

DOWN TOR:
50.5070, - 4.0033, SX 58023 69391,
What3Words: downcast.stale.survey

ALSO OF INTEREST:
Cairn circle and stone row: 50.5060, -3.9941, SX 58692 69265, What3Words: ambitions.lyricism.rock
Cuckoo Rock: 50.5010, -3.9974 SX 58470 68722 What3Words: workshops.first.sprinkler

ACCESS:
There is a car park just to the east of Norsworthy Bridge by Burrator Reservoir (What3Words: relay.reliving. freshest). From here walk directly east – there is a path – up to Down Tor. If you want to visit the stone row, continue walking east and slightly to the south to find it. (Take an Ordnance Survey map to help you navigate as it is quite hard to see until you reach it). Cuckoo Rock is also worth visiting, it is about half a mile south-west of Down Tor.

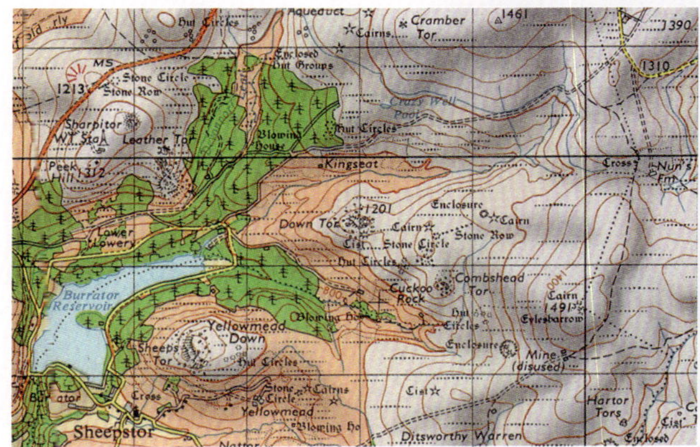

Shadows linking the stones

SHARPITOR (LUSTLEIGH)

'Sharpitor, above Lustleigh, which has also been called 'Sharp Tor' in the past, is a magnificent rockpile of epic proportions that is popular with both walkers and boulderers. It was famed for the Nutcracker Logan Rock, which was allegedly dislodged by vandals on 6th May 1950 …'

Max Piper, *East Dartmoor's Lesser-Known Tors and Rocks*, 2022

Sharpitor is one of Dartmoor's most mysterious tors. Shrouded by trees, it seems unwilling to reveal its secrets. And yet it was a top tourist spot in Victorian times, because of its famous logan stone and its extensive views of Eastern Dartmoor; back then there were no trees and its prominent position was a real draw. There is a stunning etching of it by Alfred Dawson in *An Exploration of Dartmoor and its Antiquities* (1889) by John Lloyd Warden Page, looking very different from how it appears today (see page 90).

It is now cloaked in oak and stands on a ridge overlooking Lustleigh Cleave. Cleave is the old English word for splitting along the grain, and this lush wooded gorge is on the Sticklepath Fault, an enormous geological rent in the ground created around 300 million years ago where gargantuan plates of rocks wrenched apart and moved laterally up to 10 km in opposite directions. It runs across Devon from Lundy off the north coast to Rock Walk in Torquay on the south. The constant shift of the earth's tectonic plates is written in the landscape we see here today. Sharpitor is brimming with caves, overhangs and crevices which are all on the cusp of movement; it is also surrounded by a dreamland of outlying boulders.

We visited in flaming June, climbing from the hamlet of Hammerslake. There was a tea room here until the 1930s, to service the large number of visitors in need of Darjeeling and elderflower cordial after, or indeed before, their exertions. The path off the road was narrow, with high sides; a holloway with stone steps, probably built by the Victorians to ease their passage to the attraction. Approaching the tor felt like entering a sparkling emerald plant kingdom. Although the gigantic rounded forms of the stones were everywhere they were also nowhere, submerged by creeping earth-bound understory, screened by trailing climbers, and overshadowed by the canopy. Twisted silver trunks of oak trees dripping with lichen stood silently around, and the spears of harts tongue ferns burst forth from between the boulders. It was a scene awaiting the animating fancy of a Victorian storyteller, a Conan Doyle to tell of fairies or a Tolkien to conjure hobbits.

Where to start? We couldn't see the extent of the tor at all, everything was a verdant hot mess. Soon though, a gap in the greenery focussed into a huge rock formation the size of a house with the architectural character of a grand hallway. To one side a tall convex slab leaned forward to usher us into the small arena, fitted out with a low altar-like stone (is this why the climbers call this place The Butcher's Block?). Gnarled branches formed a pierced roof over the hallway.

Pennywort spires

Donkey Cave

Horsham Bay

Leaving this place, we heard voices and a couple of walkers turned up, asking if we knew where the 'nutcrackers' were. These 'nutcrackers' are marked on the Ordnance Survey map which is unfortunately 75 years out of date. They refer to a logan stone, a stone that logs or rocks, that the tor was famed for in Victorian times. It is mentioned in an 1893 book by John Chudleigh, *Devonshire Antiquities*, who describes visiting it: '...the chief object of our search here today is the "Nutcracker" stone or Logan, near the end at which we approach the Cleave, whose presence may generally be detected by the nut shells left by enterprising tourists.'

However, the stone is no longer there; or at least, it is no longer where it used to be. In 1950, person or persons unknown knocked the stone off, causing local outrage. The Lustleigh Archives in the village contain press cuttings with headlines including: 'Lunacy at Lustleigh: Nutcracker Stone Dislodged by Vandals'. The army was even called in to try and put the stone back in its rightful place but failed when the cable they were using broke, and apparently the stone fell even further down the hill.

In fact, this wasn't the first incident of such vandalism. In 1889, John Lloyd Warden Page wrote in *An Exploration of Dartmoor and its Antiquities:* 'This logan was some years since overthrown by a visitor, gifted with more muscle than brain. I am glad to hear he was compelled to replace it, and cannot refrain from expressing a hope that the expense incurred in its restoration will prevent other mischief-lovers from attempting a like misdeed.'

In recent years many people have tried to find the fallen logan stone, but it's impossible to know which of the many boulders lying around it could be. An undated old black and white photo on the Dartmoor Trust website shows the nutcracker when it was still intact; now it is logged in memory only.

We progressed round to the southern side of the tor and clambered up among the scrub to its apex, our route in the dappled shade lit by the candle spires of pennywort flowers, growing in ranks out of the boulder stacks. Circling, we came across a large cave on the northern side, where a rocky leviathan had been sliced in two. Walking inside,

Lustleigh Cleave by Alfred Dawson

we found a large cupboard to the right which stretched quite a long way back. This feature is known as the Donkey Cave. Maybe it was used as a stable for donkeys, carrying tourists from the tea rooms to visit the tor, or maybe by woodsmen gathering fuel for their charcoal burners in the valley below.

Leaving the tor, we strolled west along the ridge, by a beautifully built old stone wall, and came across the intriguingly named Harton Chest, an enormous pillar, a granite mass with a flat top, where we sat admiring the prospect of Hound Tor, shimmering in the haze. We carried on through a grove of young oak trees, emerging into a sea of bracken, punctuated by pink foxgloves poking their heads above the tide of fronds and curls.

The next stop was the shattered rocks of Hunter's Tor, which tumble extravagantly down the side of the hill. We could see from the map that there is an Iron Age hillfort right next to it constructed from these rocks, but its outline was disguised by the green shoots of early summer. However, it was good to know it was there, even if we couldn't see it. Sitting on the top of the tor, right next to the site of a former community, we could understand why they'd chosen to live here. The tor provides a strong, natural look-out; it would also have protected them from the prevailing winds. We could see for miles around: various tors including Hay Tor and Hound Tor, and the villages of Manaton, North Bovey and Moretonhampstead. We could even see the Victorian grandeur of Bovey Castle, created by W.H.Smith of stationery fame, now a luxury hotel.

We left the ridge and walked back in a circle, heading down into the Cleave and having a plunge in the River Bovey at Horsham Bay, a grand name for a genteel, shallow pool below Horsham Steps. The latter is possibly the most unusual bridge on Dartmoor because it is entirely natural. Masses and masses of boulders lie in a huge jumble over the river which somehow manages to rush through underneath, and can only be glimpsed through a few small cracks between the rocks.

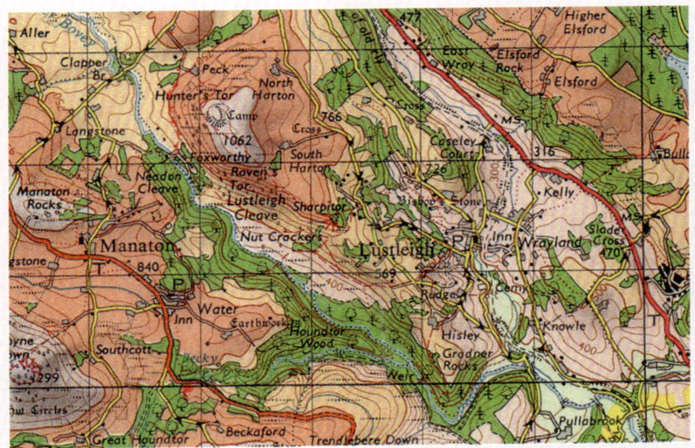

Harton Chest

SHARPITOR:
50.6200, -3.7366, SX 77278 81476
What3Words: switch.symphony.
efficient

ALSO OF INTEREST:
Harton Chest: 50.6222, -3.7440, SX 76725 81738, What3Words: radiated.retrain.doors
Hunter's Tor: 50.6287, -3.7540, SX 76035 82475 What3Words: promote.flamingo.moving
Horsham Clam: (natural boulder bridge) 50.6216, -3.75544, SX 75918 81683, What3Words: kinder.eggshell.still

ACCESS:
There are a couple of laybys on the road at the hamlet Hammerslake, very near the path to the tor. (What3Words: encrusted.connector.obscuring). From the road take the footpath west and after about two minutes walk you will reach a gate. Go through here and straight on; the tor is up ahead. After your visit, you can follow the path north-west along the ridge to find Harton Chest and Hunter's Tor. You can then continue on past Peck Farm before heading south in a circle to the river to find Horsham Steps, and from there continue in a circle back up to Harton Chest and Sharpitor.

Hunter's Tor

Greater Stitchwort

HOOKNEY TOR

'Of the tors that reside between the watersheds of the West and East Webburn Rivers, it is perhaps Hookney Tor that is the most spectacular, boasting a dominant position above the Bronze Age village of Grimspound and the lonely Headland Warren Farm. Great views are to be had from its stacks, and its location close to the minor road running southward from Challacombe Cross ensures it is frequently visited, with a wide path passing through the outcrops that is part of the long-distance Two Moors Way route'.

Paul Buck, Tim Jenkinson and Max Piper, *www.torsofdartmoor.co.uk,* 2024

Hookney Tor stands guard, like a sentry, over Dartmoor's most famous and most visited Bronze Age monument, Grimspound. Standing on the tor, looking down onto this great ring of rocks and down the combe at evidence of past farming activity, gives a powerful sense of the layering of ages onto the land, a process of (agri) cultural sedimentation on top of the wild rock. People lived here three thousand years ago, in conditions we would find hard to tolerate today. But when you think that the tor above them, which would have been a familiar part of their landscape, is hundreds of millions of years old, pre-dating the dinosaurs, that is another timescale altogether.

We headed out to visit Hookney Tor on an early July morning, which should have been the perfect time to go, but conditions were more autumnal. It had been raining solidly for the previous few days, and although it had eased off, there was a fine mizzle, the slowest form of drenching. Nevertheless, we pressed ahead with our visit, thinking it would be atmospheric in the mist, and knowing that waiting for a better day on Dartmoor is often pointless.

Mists are part and parcel of life on Dartmoor. William Crossing, in his charming book of Dartmoor walks, *Amid Devonia's Alps* (1889), has a whole chapter devoted to them, complete with some hair-raising stories of people, himself included, getting lost. In it he says: 'It is surprising how distorted objects will become in these Dartmoor mists, and how confusing is the appearance to the traveller. Small objects, close at hand (and only such as are near can be seen at all) look like large ones beheld at a distance. They will sometimes burst on the sight with almost startling suddenness, and with bewildering effect.' And large tors can be even more animated and mysterious in the mist.

On the way to Hookney Tor, we drove past the vast whale's back of Hameldown, a long dramatic ridge which is topped by several barrows, ancient burial places. Normally it dominates everything around it, but today it was invisible, shrouded in a duvet of grey mist and cloud. This valley is sparsely populated, with Challacombe Farm at the bottom and Headland Warren Farm at its head. Both are medieval in origin and on the side of Challacombe Down, above the farm, the lynchets -

Leprosy Coral Lichen

strips of land ploughed to create terraces for arable crops - are still visible, etching the hillside with deep grooves that appear in high relief on a sunny winter's day. Together, these two farms represent the diversity of modern farming on Dartmoor where the wet acidic soils mean only the adaptable survive. At Challacombe they produce beef and lamb, while Headland Warren offers holiday accommodation, and has a herd of alpacas, as well as providing space for local beekeepers.

We parked in a pull-in on the road near Headland Warren and followed an old mining gully up towards the tor. Although there was a total absence of sun, it was beautiful. We could not see very far ahead, and so paid more attention to our immediate surroundings, in particular to the vegetation we were walking through. The shocking pink of ling heather, as well as the tiny yellow dots of the tormentil flower underfoot, were welcome sparks in the gloom. Bilberry plants were everywhere, laden with fat berries which we grazed on as we passed through. Elegant brown grasses swayed in the mist, each one edged with tiny jewels of dew.

We reached the top of the gulley and hiked along the ridge towards the tor which we knew was nearby but which we could not yet see. The wind was much stronger here on the top, and we also had to contend with a constant flow of moist mizzle swirling past. Suddenly, a rock loomed up in the mist, followed by other, bigger blocks popping up ahead. We had arrived at Hookney Tor.

It was an archipelago in a ghostly sea. There were at least six separate piles. Many of the rocks were covered in a pale grey, almost white lichen, *Lepra corallina*, leprosy coral lichen, growing in large crusty splashes. They seemed to glow in the half-light. The largest stack reared up like a behemoth from the depths, with a stumpy neck in the middle; it was in two parts, with an empty blow hole in between, which formed a kind of tall thin space in which we stood and sheltered from the elements. We walked around the back of the neck and found a series of natural steps, like a small staircase, leading to the top. It felt like ascending to the bridge of a ship to peer anxiously into the fog.

We knew Grimspound was a short distance below the tor but we couldn't see it. We went in its direction down the hill, following a path made of flat granite flags. Ahead, the mist covered the top of Challacombe Down, but the early morning sun had lit the valley from underneath and the small road to Widecombe appeared below, a thin silver line against the vivid green fields.

At the same time, Grimspound suddenly came into view, at this distance a delicate circle of stone that seemed to float in the blurry moorland scenery, like the footprint of some alien spaceship. As we approached, it disappeared, and then appeared again, as the mist came and went. Finally, up close, its great boundary wall sprawled over Grim's

Grimspound entrance

Grimspound by Alfred Dawson, 1889

Lake stream. These double-skinned walls were once nearly 2m high, but have been displaced by thousands of years of weather and gravity.

Grimspound dates from the late Bronze Age (about 1500-800 BC). It was the home of some of the first farmers on Dartmoor, with the remains of over 20 round houses, or hut circles, whose foundations can be seen today. In a land covered in low scrub and woodland, they grew their crops and farmed livestock, bringing them in behind the pound's massive walls at night, protected from wolves and bears.

The site was first excavated in the last decade of the nineteenth century, by the wonderfully named Dartmoor Exploration Committee, a group of gentlemen antiquarians who included Sabine Baring-Gould and Robert Burnard. Archaeology was a relatively new discipline, and they went on to investigate many more of Dartmoor's neolithic monuments, including stone rows, hut circles and stone circles.

There are some evocative black and white photographs of them hard at work at Grimspound in 1894. They excavated numerous round houses (the remains of which are called hut circles) and found paved floors, charcoal, cooking holes and hearths. They restored some of the houses 'although not very accurately', according to English Heritage, which now looks after the site. Often their work is regarded by the experts nowadays as clumsy and interventionist, but there is no doubt that if it had not been for these curious Victorian antiquarians, many more of Dartmoor's fascinating monuments would have been lost, exposed to the elements, and also to the dry stone wallers and the road menders.

At the time the amateur archaeologists were busy, Dartmoor was getting well developed as a tourist destination, with growing numbers of guidebooks. John Lloyd Warden Page, in *An Exploration of Dartmoor and its Antiquities* (1889) writes evocatively of Grimspound, as well as providing a beautiful illustration (see page 95).

We meandered around the outside of the enormous wall, following the circle around to the grand entrance to the village on the south-eastern side. A party of hikers appeared, walking down from Hameldown; we followed them through the gateway (you can never visit Grimspound without finding other people there). The other group settled in the most complete hut circle to eat their lunch while we wandered around, trying to imagine this place in its heyday. Smoke would have drifted from cooking pots through the thatched roofs of the little dwellings, the long-horned cattle would have been bellowing in their pens, and dirty children would have been running around, mouths blue from eating bilberries, playing hide and seek at the tor.

On a clearer day, we would have continued our walk up onto the grand ridge of Hameldown, to explore its tor and numerous cairns, as well as to admire the views. This is highly recommended, but only when there is good visibility.

Grimspound

Hut circle, Grimspound

HOOKNEY TOR:
50.6163, -3.8412, SX 69834 81225, What3Words: consults.moisture.friends

ALSO OF INTEREST:
Grimspound: 50.6132, -3.8378, SX 70062 80895, What3Words: giggles.objective.hunt
Hameldown Tor: 50.6104, -3.8342, SX 70313 80574, What3Words: slipped.clerk.ounce

ACCESS:
Park on a pull-in by the minor road near Headland Warren Farm (What3Words: steepest.verve.lied). From here, follow the gully north-east and then pick up the path heading south to Hookney Tor. From here continue south to Grimspound. You can extend the walk by carrying on south-east from Grimspound to Hameldown Tor, and then along Hameldown to see several barrows and boundary stones.

HEN TOR

'Hen Tor (1,325 feet) is a striking part of Plym's middle-reach scenery. Its giant cone, so often dark in appearance, protrudes boldly from Hentor Hill on the side of the Plym Ridge rising three hundred feet above it. Spreading fanwise from its north west foot is one of the most remarkable clitters on Dartmoor…They lie in an amazing series of rock-streams which, from the summit of the tor, appear as an unusual foreground to a varied and fascinating view.'

Eric Hemery, *High Dartmoor,* 1983

Hen Tor is not the easiest of tors to reach, but its remoteness is part of its stern character. There are no trees up here; none can survive the full force of the gales coming in from the Atlantic. It has a weird feeling of both emptiness and presence. It is as though the tor, with its inky grey volcanic core and billows of surrounding clitter, is the eye of one of those storms that has arrived here and petrified. This impression of an empty space made solid is reinforced by the 3-mile walk to it, past the epic craters of the Lee Moor china clay pits, massive man-made voids which perch on the rim of the moor before it drops away to the sea at Plymouth Sound.

On an early July morning, the skies were blue and it was warm, but with a strong northerly wind which kept us cool as we walked. Shortly after leaving the car park, we passed Blackaton Cross, a medieval stone waymarker. The road by which it stands was a major route across Dartmoor in the Middle Ages; now it goes nowhere, leading into the empty air above the clay pits. The white alps of the mines loomed in the distance over to the south-east, with an orange dumper truck trundling around on the top of the spoil like one of the orange Cardinal beetles in the grass beneath our feet. For every tonne of china clay that is extracted, four tonnes of white mica and sand are left behind, making up these mountains of the moon.

As we approached Big Pond, which supplies water for the quarry, swifts bombed back and forth over our heads, swooping into the sparkling surface every so often to drink. The pond, which is fenced off with lots of official warning signs from the quarry authorities, is fed by a leat which was built around two hundred years ago. Its purpose was to feed the water streams and jets that scoured away the sides of the pit, carrying away thousands of tonnes of china clay over the years into the enormous settling tanks below.

Occupied with the task of industrial extraction for good profits, the builders of this leat, back in early Victorian times, were not concerned about the minor inconvenience of a prehistoric double stone row which was standing minding its own business nearby, as it had done for the previous three thousand years. The labourers built the leat straight through the middle of it. The whole row could have been destroyed, but fortunately it survived, thanks to a parson from Plympton, the Rev W J Coppard, who happened to be passing and witnessed the destruction of human history in full flow. In a report in the Archaeological Journal of 1860, he described how he saw 'a party of navvies' who were 'carrying off some of the stones from the avenue which was near at hand, and had blasted some of them with gunpowder'. He alerted the local squire and managed to stop any further destruction. A hundred years later, in 1961, a nearby row was not so lucky and was fully sacrificed to the china clay industry. The 217-metre-long Cholwich Town Stone Row is now buried deep under the pits; it was destroyed by mining, although it was excavated first. Who knows how many more 'ghost monuments' there are in Dartmoor's mines and pits.

Given enough time though, all stones on Dartmoor will become ghosts. The clay pits only exist because granite has decomposed over millions of years into a magical white powder: china clay. Also called kaolin, it is valued for its use in everything from making paper white, to the pellets that make No 10's doors bomb-proof. Most famously, it has been highly prized for hundreds of years for making fine translucent white porcelain ceramics and sculptures, after being first discovered at Mount Kao-ling in China. Who knows, perhaps fragments of the Cholwich Town Stone Row have already been resurrected as Wedgewood shepherdesses, or a delicate Worcester tea service, or perhaps a gleaming white toilet by Armitage Shanks.

At the end of the Big Pond, we turned around to look at the vast mine workings before us, like a sort of lost world. We then followed the leat north-west to find the double stone row (known today as the Trowlesworthy Row), which was aligned north-south, with the leat cutting through it at the southern end. The stones were large and it felt complete, despite the ravages of the past, and

Trowlesworthy double stone row

Bone offering, Hen Tor

Lee Moor china clay pits

Big Pond

the watercourse bisecting it. As we walked along the row, we could see a trio of crows standing on a nearby rock. As we approached the cairn circle at the northern end of the row, which is known as The Pulpit, one of them flew over and perched on the most unusual stone in the circle, which is shaped like an arrowhead with a narrow neck. As we got there it flew off, but we could see the stone had been baptised in a purple guano of half-digested ivy berries; obviously an ancient perching post for generations of corvids.

Continuing past Great Trowlesworthy Tor, we nearly stepped on a young, diamond-backed adder as we explored around its boulders. From there we followed Willings Wall, a prehistoric reave, or ancient boundary marker, built in the Middle Bronze Age approximately 3500 years ago. We stopped for a cup of lapsang souchong tea and a shortbread biscuit on a big rock near the wall and noticed a kistvaen nearby. Its large stone lid was to one side, indicating it had probably been robbed in the past, but the square stone coffin-like box was still very much intact.

By now we could see Hen Tor in the distance, three distinct piles, with a huge amount of clitter in front of it, a fountain of rock. Fat grey clouds started to gather above us, blocking out the light and darkening the tor. As we got closer, we could see that the central core did indeed look like a hen: a fat one, sitting down, like one of those china egg containers people have in their kitchens, depicting a chicken on a nest. As we got nearer, the impression of a hen faded, as the tor metamorphosed into a stumpy cargo ship sailing forth in granite seas; its northern end like a prow. At its southern end it was possible to climb up it and sit in an alcove at the top, just like being on the deck of a ship, looking down at the rock shoals below.

Sitting there, we thought also about the many people who lived and worked in this small corner of Dartmoor in the past. Up until the middle of the nineteenth century, there was a farm immediately below and to the west of the tor, and thousands of years before that, our Bronze Age predecessors made many homes here. They all transformed the stone from the clitter into their dwellings, fragments of which remain today and can be found in the form of old foundations and hut circles. As we made our way down the slopes of the tor, we marvelled at the power the old stones have to shape-shift. The forces of nature slowly change their massive forms, they metamorphose in our imaginations into megalithic connectors to the spirit world, and are eventually transformed into china clay that can be modelled in the palms of our hands into both everyday utensils and as yet un-dreamt of ceramic creations.

Kistvaen

INFORMATION

HEN TOR:
50.4706, -3.9835, SX 59336 65304, What3Words: incensed.plays.cashier

ALSO OF INTEREST:
Big Pond: 50.4514, -4.0078, SX 57554 63213, What3Words: cyber.helping.spellings
Cairn circle and double stone row: 50.4582, -4.0067, SX 57647 63975, What3Words: successes.waistcoat.tabloid
Trowlesworthy Tors: 50.4615, -4.0023, SX 57970 64326, What3Words: recipient.condiment.flippers
Ruins of Hen Tor Farm: 50.4729, -3.9884, SX 58994 65569 What3Words: himself.courts.collect

ACCESS:
There is a car park by the china clay pits (What3Words: inhabited.imitate.coconuts). It's a walk of about 3 miles to the tor. You will need an Ordnance Survey map. Head east with the pits on your right, passing Big Pond on your right. Then head north along the leat, where you will find the double stone row and cairn circle, before heading north-east up to Great Trowlesworthy Tor. From here you need to keep heading north-east to find Hen Tor (use your map to navigate the rest of the way.)

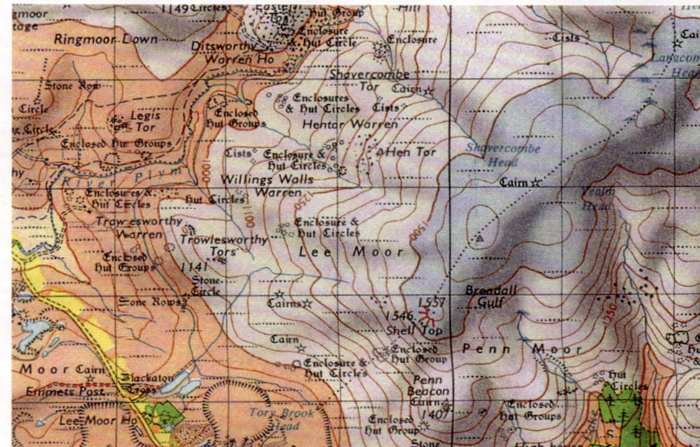

The Pulpit

CROCKERN TOR

'The tor stands on the north rim of the Central Basin and, practically speaking, is the centre of the Dartmoor medieval tin-streaming area; consequently, the boundaries of the four stannary districts of Devon radiate from it. The trans-Dartmoor packhorse track (Central Basin north) touches its very foot, no other tor of comparable size being so near the track: it was, therefore a significant landmark for the traveller.'

Eric Hemery, *High Dartmoor*, 1983

Crockern Tor is one of the most famous tors on Dartmoor; not so much for its physical stature, but for being a place where politics, protest, and legend collide. A drawing of it features in an 1826 long-form verse by N T Carrington, *Dartmoor: A Descriptive Poem* (see page 106). For several centuries, between the Middle Ages and the early eighteenth century, it was the location of an open-air court, called the Stannary Parliament. This was the governing body of the tin industry that answered only to the Crown, which met to resolve disputes and administer justice. It is thought that the spot was chosen because of its location right in the middle of the moor, between the stannary towns of Tavistock, Chagford, Ashburton and Plympton.

If that were not remarkable enough, the tor is also associated with a legendary figure known as 'Old Crockern', said to be the spirit or father of Dartmoor. Sabine Baring-Gould, in his *Book of the West*, (1899) described him as 'the gurt old sperit of the moors, old Crockern himself, grey as granite, and his eyebrows hanging down over his glimmering eyes like sedge, and his eyes deep as peat water pools.' This terrifying figure rode a skeleton horse over the tors at night, defending the moor from anyone who wished to exploit it, particularly landowners.

The idea of 'Old Crockern' has recently been revived by the Right to Roam campaign, which has invoked him as the figurehead for their movement to resist attempts to ban wild camping on Dartmoor and increase access rights. Channelling ancient folk traditions, he dances at the front of protest marches, personified in an impressive towering costume of green and brown rags, with a sculpted, craggy rocky face like that of the tor itself.

One of Old Crockern's haunts is said to be Wistman's Wood, less than a mile from the tor, and another of Dartmoor's most weird features. A small ancient temperate rainforest, full of dwarf oaks, it is a fragment left over from when trees covered most of Dartmoor after the last ice age. It is perhaps this sense of being a relic, and its fairytale appearance, that has made it the subject of wild fantasies over hundreds of years, home to nests of writhing adders, a grove of the Druids, and the kennels of the notorious wisht hounds.

We had a reminder that rights of access to the moor are by permission only, as we followed the track from Two Bridges to Wistmans Wood, passing several official Duchy of Cornwall signs

Crockern Tor by P. H. Rogers.

Parliament Rock

Sessile oaks, Wistmans Wood

View from Parliament Rock south

on the gates to bordering fields. Each one had the Duchy's black and white coat of arms, and bore the legend 'no public access'. A huge part of Dartmoor has been owned by the monarchy since Saxon times; the Duchy was established in 1337 by Edward III, as an endowment for his son the Prince of Wales. Its biggest landholding then, and now, is Dartmoor, where it owns over 67,000 acres, and provides an income of millions of pounds for Prince William.

We could see the West Dart flowing along beside us, a short distance to the west, surrounded by mires, and, further to the west on top of the next ridge, the rocky eminence of Beardown Tors. The red flag was flying on top, warning of live firing in the Merrivale Range further to the west. Looking up into the valley, the rocky river snaked into the distance and the moor was a sea of lush green new grasses. Up ahead we could see the dark green patch of the wood clinging to the eastern side of the valley, just above the river.

Ahead of the wood, we arrived at a stile and were greeted by a further array of official notices. Two from Natural England welcomed us to Wistman's Wood and told us to 'walk around not through' and the other was a scarlet FIRE RISK sign. Five minutes later, we reached the southern border of the wood and were relieved to find it was not fenced off. We had feared it might be, after years of news reports about the destruction caused by people and sheep.

There were a couple of groups of people there, all respecting the request to stay out. Sitting on a mossy boulder at the edge, we peered into the green, dappled world of the wood. Small twisted branches stretched out like arms, linking in a low, crooked canopy. Ferns, brackens and lichens were everywhere, covering the rocks under the trees and the trees themselves. Groups of white star-shaped flowers, English stonecrop, clustered in the moss on some of the boulders. We found a large, flat rock, rather like an altar, just to the side of the trees, and lay down on it and shut our eyes, listening to hover flies buzzing around us and finches chattering in the branches, and feeling the gentle breeze wafting over our bodies.

We carried on around the eastern side of the wood and, just before it petered out, noticed what

Buller's Rock

looked like a large standing stone on the edge. We climbed down to look at it and discovered it was inscribed, saying: 'By permission of HRH The Prince of Wales, Wentworth Buller on Sept 16th 1868 cut down a tree near this spot it measured 9 inches in diameter and appeared to be about 163 years old'. The lettering was very beautifully carved but hard to read. Why had Wentworth Buller cut down the tree? Presumably to measure its age. And why had he gone to the trouble of recording these facts on a stone for all to see? Perhaps visitors did not believe these naturally small sessile oaks could be so old, so once it was proved, Wentworth decided to settle all future arguments with the authority of stone.

Leaving the wood behind, we hiked up to the ridge to the east to Littaford Tors and walked south to Crockern Tor. As we approached, we could see the trans-moor road running ahead into the distance, and the choice of the tor as the open-air meeting place for the tinners made a lot of sense. Perched on the edge of the ridge, the tor seemed the monarch of all it surveyed. We picked our way through large areas of clitter to find the tor's main feature, Parliament Rock, said to be where the Lord Warden would have stood and made his pronouncements. It was the most striking natural feature, a large, fat pillar with natural steps up the back. Alongside it, on a ledge, was a series of large blocks which Eric Hemery, in *High Dartmoor*, argues would have been seats for the court officials. 'Perched, in the form of a coping, along the ledge which extends from the lower portion of Parliament Rock, are several slabs of great size. They appear primarily to have been the result of frost partings in the ledge, the upper face of which has a natural slope. Smaller blocks of stone have been inserted beneath each in such a way as to raise it, and so afford a level upper surface. The result is a kind of balcony, which would have seated, or provided a long table for, at least eight clerks or officials.'

We stood on Parliament Rock and tried to imagine what a meeting here would have been like. Horses and ponies would have been tethered near the roadside while about a hundred medieval miners, streamers, beamers, captains, crushers, crazers and stampers would have rubbed shoulders with local dignitaries and farmers. Most would have sat beneath the rock, to hear the disputes of the tinners and the proclamations of the judge. To our modern selves, it seems an extraordinary place to conduct business. And yet, in recent times, people have congregated here, feeling the pull of the stone in this natural amphitheatre; in 2015, at the time of a UN climate summit, over a hundred people marched to the tor carrying the figure of a polar bear, calling for a cleaner planet. We think the spirit of Old Crockern was looking over their shoulder that time too, standing up against those who want to despoil the moor directly or indirectly.

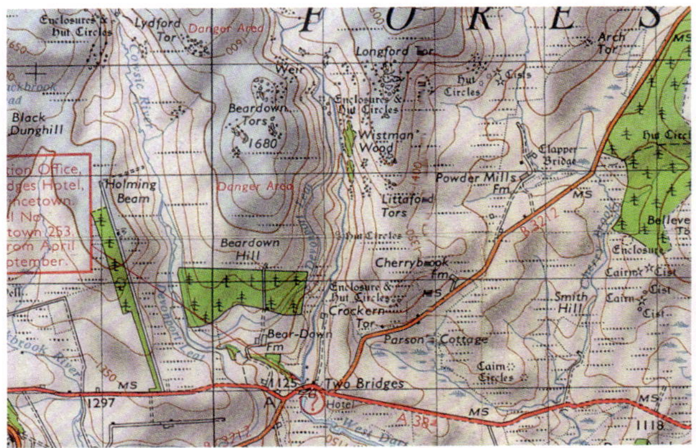

Littaford Tors

CROCKERN TOR:

50.5653, -3.9561, SX 61560 75778, What3Words: prancing.succumbs.dignity

ALSO OF INTEREST:

Wistman's Wood: 50.5763, -3.9611, SX 61233 77018, What3Words: emptied.thatched.feed

Littaford Tors: 50.5774, -3.9563, SX 61578 77134, What3Words: lads.noses.ramp

ACCESS:

Car park at Two Bridges (What3Words: connector.unheated.cunning). Crockern Tor is about a mile from the car park. Follow the track north for about half a mile until you get to a farmhouse. Bear right and then head east, walking through a gap in a stone wall, to find Crockern Tor. If you want to include Wistman's Wood in your walk follow the same route but at the farmhouse continue walking north with the river on your left, to find the wood. Then head directly east up the hill to Littaford Tors which sit on top of the ridge. From here, head directly south along the ridge to find Crockern Tor. (This walk is about 4 miles).

Wistman's Wood

CALVESLAKE TOR

'...we...shall make our way to Calves Lake Tor, a small pile ½ mile distant. Very near to this on the SE is a kistvaen, the covering slab of which has been raised, and now hangs partly over the open grave...having crossed the Plym at Calves Lake Foot we find ourselves close to another little tributary, which comes down from Evil Combe.'

William Crossing, *Guide to Dartmoor,* 1912

Calveslake Tor is a secret to the casual observer. There is not much talk of it by other writers on Dartmoor. It is of no great height, and does not top a hill, but is buttered on the side of Crane Hill just above the River Plym. And yet, it is truly special. Its remote setting, not far from one of the most breathtaking prehistoric ritual sites on Dartmoor, is a huge plus. It is covered with a jungle of lichens thriving in the pollution-free moorland air, and, best of all, it has a logan stone that actually logs, a rare thing indeed.

It was a windy summer's day, with constantly changing skies, as we embarked on our trek. Arriving below the ragged silhouette of Gutter Tor, not far from Sheepstor, we had a steady climb of about one and a half miles up a track past several short granite obelisks marking the catchment area of Burrator Reservoir, which was created in 1898 by drowning the Meavy valley. Paul Rendell, in his book *Exploring Around Burrator* (2023), explains there are at least 71 of these stones in the area, each bearing the letters PCWW – Plymouth Corporation Water Works – as well as the dates 1917, 1919, or 1932, indicating the years the land was bought.

We passed the extensive ruins of Eylesburrow Mine, which was worked for tin for a few decades of the early nineteenth century. Two hundred years ago this was a busy industrial area, with mine shafts burrowing deep into the hillside. Underground, the tinners followed seams of sparkling cassiterite formed in metamorphic rock as the molten magma squeezed through ancient sea beds here 280 million years ago. Overground, there was a smelting house, stamping mills, a blacksmith's shop, and accommodation for the workers. The ruins of many of the buildings are still visible today, notably a rather surreal section of wall with a window in the middle, standing in isolation like a forgotten bit of film set. This is all that remains of the wheelpit of Stamping Mill 2, where the mined ore was finely crushed (or crazed as they would say in the West Country).

We also noticed what looked like a double stone row, although from a previous visit knew that it wasn't in fact prehistoric, but also a relic of the tin mine. The stones were part of a so-called flatrod system of wooden or iron rods, which linked a waterwheel to the mine shafts. As the waterwheel turned, it pushed the flatrods which in turn powered the underground pumps at the mineshafts further up the hill.

Leaving the mine behind, we noticed a large herd of snorting Dartmoor ponies with spider-

Logan stone

legged foals heading straight for us. One was branded with the letter W. A quick ascent up the side of the track let them pass; as semi-wild ponies, they weren't wearing shoes and made surprisingly little noise, just soft drumming on the springy peat as they cantered by, their dark flanks dappling in the sun. As they disappeared into the distance, a solitary heron flew overhead. We headed east, enjoying the gloriously spacious panorama that spread before us: green moorland, huge skies, no trees, enormous clouds. It felt like entering a world with no end; a place away from our everyday concerns.

Next was a descent into Evil Combe, a gully leading down to the River Plym. This cratered little valley, like the ruins we'd just passed, is also the result of humans raiding the earth for resources; in this instance, our medieval ancestors streaming for tin. According to Eric Hemery, in *High Dartmoor*, there is no sinister reason for the name: an 'evil' is the miners' name for an iron pick. Saying that, we did find a lamb's skull lying at the bottom of the valley, an involuntary sacrifice by lamb, herd and farmer to a hard life on the moor.

The bubbling River Plym, its waters sparkling in the sun, was the next obstacle to navigate, and we bog-hopped towards Calves Lake which was the last hurdle between us and the tor. The word 'lake' on Dartmoor actually means a stream, and in this instance, a tiny one, but which nevertheless still proved difficult to cross because of the quaking sphagnum mire all around it. Eventually, we got over with dry feet and ascended the gentle slope towards Calveslake Tor.

Threading our way through smooth, swollen boulders dotted all over the hillside, we approached the tor. The overall impression was of soft organic bulbousness, unlike other precipitous tors which are often surrounded by jagged clitter. The tor itself was low and friendly, with rounded edges clinging to the contours of the hill. Soft wetness also overflowed around one of the main outcrops, surrounded by rushes and spongy ground. Scooped out by water and ice it contained a hollow which went a long way back, its dark inner crevices lined with a visceral purple mould. Another, higher pile, had an elongated, protruding stone, scaled with lichen and moss, which looked like the snout of one of the diamond-backed adders we have occasionally stumbled across near here.

Many of the rocks were adorned with a dark, pustule-like lichen, covering them like an astrakhan coat. We see lichens all the time on Dartmoor but their seemingly infinite variety, minute detail and uncanny colour elude and confuse. We got out our *Guide to Lichens of Heaths and Moors*, from the Field Studies Council, and came to the conclusion it was *Lasallia pustulata* or blistered navel lichen, although

Lichen covered boulder

Bone Stone, Drizzlecombe

we couldn't be sure. We were, however, content to bask in the lichens' weird radiance without having to name them.

As we explored the tor, we pushed on the rocks to see if they moved, hoping to find a logan stone which we'd read about on the *Tors of Dartmoor* website. Logan stones, rocking or logging stones, are the stuff of legend on Dartmoor. They are stones that can be wobbled but don't fall down (we love Weebles – google it); they are often perched at precarious angles. Much mythology has grown up around them, including that they were the instruments of the Druids who were able to show their power by moving the immovable with just a single finger.

In Victorian times, they were great attractions, visited by charabancs full of tourists armed with nuts, keen to crack them under the logan stone. Indeed, there are many still marked on the Ordnance Survey map today, even though many have been knocked off their perch or no longer rock. Despite their prevalence on the map, we have never found a functioning one. Many have been vandalised for fun over the years, or simply fallen.

So we were very excited to find, at the top of the tor, a long flat rock that stood like an egg on a plate, and actually moved with a simple push of the hand. Stone in motion feels awe-inspiring, the deep cavernous sound of stone on stone, its weight making it feel inexorable, skittish and potentially lethal, reminding us of our soft bodies and thin bones. A short distance to the south of the tor was another stone reminder of our soft bodies. Here we found a large kistvaen, an ancient grave, its granite lid at a jaunty 45-degree angle where grave robbers in search of bronze had levered it up.

With some reluctance we left the tor, still buoyed up by the logan stone discovery, to cross the river valley again and head for Drizzlecombe to pay homage to the largest menhir on Dartmoor and its radiating stone rows. The ceremonial complex has three rows aligned north-east south-west, each with a terminal stone at one end and a cairn grave at the other. One has an enormous terminal stone called the Bone Stone, which stands over four metres tall, its round head accounting for its name. There are also four other cairns and a kist around it, including a huge one to the side called the Giant's Basin.

To the north, east and west are the remains of the teeming villages that built this place of the spirit and the stones. It is interesting though that the hut circles to the north-east are considerably smaller than normal; some archeologists believe they were shelters used by young people who were sent out to look after the livestock in the summer months.

We approached the monuments from this way, stopping at the brow of the hill, among these ruined hut circles, to look down at the network of megaliths and cairns in its entirety, the lines of the rows converging towards us. They stood in a wide plain with the Plym bordering them on the eastern side, powerfully still in the heat haze. Slowly we processed south-west along the rows, past the ponies leaning against the stones, pondering the imponderable. What were these crowds of stone for, how did people relate to them, what visions did the builders see and what stories of people and the moor did they tell when they gathered here?

Leaving the rows behind, we passed the faceless shell of Ditsworthy Warren Farm, long abandoned. In 2011 it was used as a set for the film *Warhorse* by Steven Spielberg, a modern story of the moors, in which a horse and a farm boy were sent to a terrible war.

CALVESLAKE TOR:
50.4918, -3.9636, SX 60806 67627
What3Words: plausible.suffix.holds

ALSO OF INTEREST:
Eylesburrow Mine remains: 50.4964, -3.9782, SX 59790 68168
What3Words: compress.dressings.layover
Drizzlecombe Stone Rows: 50.4858, -3.9859, SX 59206 66999
What3Words: casually.pound.wrenching

ACCESS:
Park at Gutter Tor car park (What3Words: steady.encodes.churn). Calveslake Tor is about 2.5 miles from the car park. From here, head towards the outward-bound centre surrounded by trees. Follow the track uphill north-east for 1.5 miles to find the old mine remains. Just after the mine remains take the right-hand fork and then turn right off the track to walk down Evil Combe. Cross the river and then head south-east to find Calveslake Tor. Go back the way you came or else, from the tor, head south-east, crossing the river again, to visit the Drizzlecombe stone rows. From here you can walk back to the car past Ditsworthy Warren House and then take the track north-west from there back to the car park.

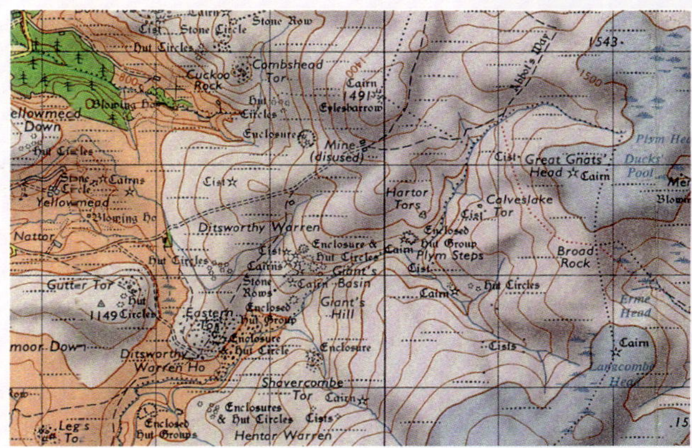

River Plym

Blistered Navel Lichen

Vesuvius Snow Lichen

Powdered Ruffle Lichen

VIXEN TOR

'...we shall observe Vixen Tor, not forming the crest of an eminence as is more frequently the case, but rising majestically from the common...On a nearer approach, we shall remark the resemblance which it bears to the Egyptian Sphynx, when beheld from a particular point of view. Fronting the river, the huge masses of which the tor is composed are piled up tier after tier, in a rude but noble façade...this lofty rock is traditionally reported to have been resorted to in past times for astronomical purposes.'

Samuel Rowe, *A Perambulation of the Antient and Royal Forest of Dartmoor,* 1856

For over twenty years Vixen Tor has been barred to the public. In 2003, its then-new owner, Mary Alford, decided to close it off, concerned about being liable for any accidents suffered by visitors. Many, including the Ramblers Association, the Open Spaces Society, and Devon County Council challenged the decision, but in 2011, after eight years of disputes, mass trespasses, and legal wrangles, including two public inquiries, Mary Alford won her battle to keep the public out.

It is still possible to admire this hypnotically compelling tor from the wall that borders it, although the experience is sullied by barbed wire and various 'keep out' signs. It's all very sad, as for well over two centuries, in fact ever since people started to visit Dartmoor, Vixen Tor has been regarded as one of the area's finest natural treasures and has been consistently mentioned in the literature. At about 30 metres high, it is the tallest tor on Dartmoor, and its uncanny shapes have given rise to stories and legends, not least that of Vixiana the Witch, who lives in a cave at its foot and lures unsuspecting ramblers to their deaths in the bogs that surround it.

The weather forecast was predicting temperatures of 29 degrees Celsius with clear skies, so we decided to head out early to avoid the heat of the midday sun; the high moors can shimmer with heat in the high summer, the mirages rippling the shadeless grasslands like a pond. It was just after 7:30 am when we started walking over Whitchurch Common; the early light gave everything a luminosity and the sky directly above was that sharp cobalt blue that starts at the edge of space. Thankfully, there was already a welcome breeze coming from the sparkling waters of Plymouth Sound. Vixen Tor was clearly visible, a prominent bulk and familiar landmark in the local scenery, sitting as it does less than half a mile from the tourist road. After ten minutes' walk, we quickly reached the earth and stone wall which is the nearest viewing point for the tor.

'No Public Access' was scrawled in pulsing red paint over a large, millions of years old, lichen-covered outlier of Vixen Tor that had been incorporated into the wall. Festoons of barbed wire were woven across the face of it. There was another sign, again daubed in red paint on a nearby boulder, saying 'No Access'. Just in case anyone was in any doubt, further north along the wall, there was a five-bar metal gate, fortified with barbed wire and an extra layer of wire cage, with, again, 'No Access' painted in bloody red on the gatepost. The message couldn't be clearer: stay out. Despite this, there were signs of rebellion. Someone had placed part of an old wooden pallet on the barbed wire, creating a makeshift step up onto the granite outcrop to aid trespassers.

The imprisoned tor stood about 100 metres behind the wall, looking both smaller and more insignificant than it had appeared from further away, and at the same time contemptuous of the tawdry man-made interventions around it. It made us feel uncomfortable, its weighted, calm presence spoilt by squeals of human discord.

Ignoring the signs and barbed wire, we focussed on the tor, a pyramid of rock surrounded by small gnarled hawthorn trees. From where we were standing, the pile resembled the two-faced god Janus: two faces in profile, back-to-back. This was perhaps appropriate as he is the god of gates and thresholds, and we felt this reflected the atmosphere of the place.

Vixen Tor has been known locally as the Sphinx since at least the 19th century, when postcards were produced of it, emphasising the human profile of its apex and the outstretched boulders like a lion's paws. Although in Egyptian mythology the Sphinx is a benevolent guardian that symbolises strength, in Greek mythology it is a vicious and merciless creature, a lion with the head of a woman and wings of an eagle, that kills and eats travellers that do not answer a riddle it asks. This is interesting as this image may have grown from another legend about Vixen Tor, which also features a brutish woman, a witch called Vixiana, who also traps unwary visitors.

Vixiana, (whose name is, of course, taken from a female fox; some say this is also what the tor looks like), commanded an array of pixies and will o' the wisps who lived with her in her cave under the tor. They helped her to trap and drown passers-by in the bogs, lost in the fog she conjured. She was eventually defeated and killed by a handsome young Dartmoor man, just as the Sphinx was defeated by the beautiful but flawed Oedipus. We wondered if we should actually feel sorry for Vixiana; witches generally get a bad press, and maybe she just wanted some peace and quiet. Perhaps it is not surprising that these eddies of myth still swirl about the place today, as travellers are still repelled and occupiers demonised.

We followed the wall south, passing more red signs painted on stones, and started to see a very different aspect of the tor. From here, it appeared much larger and grander, like a castle, with great ramparts flying up from the ground: more mountainous, less singular. Behind it, in the distance, stood Great Mis Tor. Continuing south, the ground got wetter, and rounding the corner of the field wall we were surprised to see a tawny owl lifting off from a large boulder, stretching the short night's hunting time into the early morning. As it drifted silently away into the oaks of the Walkham valley we hiked up towards Heckwood Tor, passing another sign, this time for Heckwood Farm, which bore the legend 'Bull Roaming'. Another, not-so-subtle, message to the great unwashed to keep out, although this sign was at least carved tastefully in wood.

Heckwood Tor is spread in a series of outcrops along the top of a ridge, and includes a precisely poised, monumental jointed pillar which we could see would once have been even taller; the top of it had fallen off and lay on one side. Sitting at the

Standing stone in front of Vixen Tor

summit of the tor felt like being at the epicentre of a granite amphitheatre. We were surrounded by an arc of tors, mauve-blue in the distance: Cox Tor, Great Staple Tor, Great Mis Tor, Vixen Tor, Kings Tor, Leeden Tor, Ingra Tor and Sharpitor.

As we headed south-west towards Pew Tor, the ground was littered with many stones that had been worked. We'd noticed, at Heckwood Tor, that some of the boulders bore feather and tare marks – regular notches in the stone – indicating that at some point in the past, someone had split some of the rock off. There was a lot of quarrying for granite here in the nineteenth century, with stone being used, among other things, for the building of Plymouth's Breakwater. The extraction continued well into the twentieth century; just nearby, the massive gouge in the hillside that is Merrivale Quarry only closed in 1997.

Our next stop was a pool in an old pit a short distance south-west of Pew tor. By now it was sweltering and we were longing for a swim. The water was opaque, a bright olive green from algae proliferating in the intense sunlight; harmless (although not the most attractive) and very refreshing in the heat. A fellow walker told us that there was once an animal rescue here, in similarly hot weather. Apparently, the water level got so low that the fish were in danger. The RSPCA were called and removed them to safety. Of course, there was torrential rain the next day.

We retraced our steps back over Pew Tor where we found a pink Tupperware box which turned out to be Dartmoor Letterbox No 50662. It contained a stamp in memory of Kate Hatherell who died of an asthma attack in 2017, aged 31. A laminated card explained that she grew up in Plymouth and spent many happy times at Pew Tor as a child. Our hearts went out to the Hatherells, and we left them a message in the notebook, sending our love and also mentioning our dear son Felix who died, aged 20, in the same year.

Wandering slowly onwards towards Windy Cross, we could see cattle gathering around it. The cross is a medieval way marker positioned by the Grimstone and Sortridge Leat. It is finer than many Dartmoor crosses, having chamfered edges. We were intrigued by a so-called 'bullseye stone' in the wall of the leat: a hole the size of – you've guessed it - a bullseye, siphoning off water into another channel. There are several 'bullseyes' in this leat; they were a simple way of diverting water, and could easily be blocked up with turf if required.

By now, Vixen Tor was in view again in the distance, a symbol of the conflict on Dartmoor between who controls the land, and who has access to it. In the twentieth century, there were bitter battles over the creation of public assets like conifer forests and reservoirs; in the twenty-first century, there are equally passionate debates – and legal cases – over public access and where people have the right to go. Perhaps, in future, peace will break out, curses will be lifted, and Vixen Tor will be set free again.

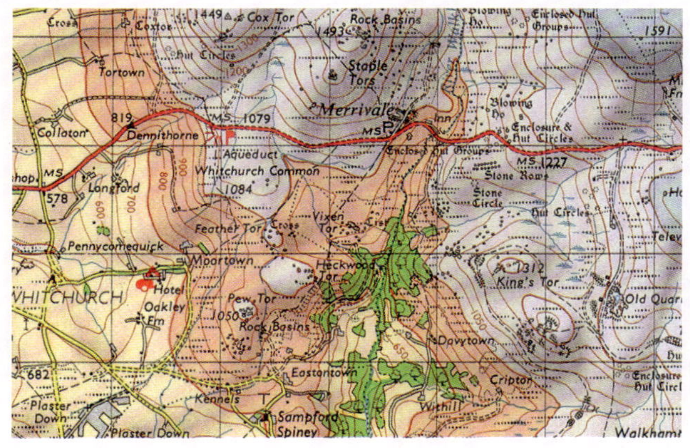

Vixen Tor from the south

VIXEN TOR:
50.5497, -4.0591, SX 54214 74244,
What3Words: hoped.encroach.prestige

ALSO OF INTEREST:
Heckwood Tor: 50.5456, -4.0652, SX 53769 73798, What3Words: putts.loved.sooner
Pew Tor: 50.5424, -4.0725, SX 53245 73461, What3Words: blush.tells.budgeted
Old quarry pool: 50.5397, -4.0742, SX 53112 73160, What3Words: whisker.admires originate
Bullseye Stone: 50.5499, -4.0699, SX 53447 74295, What3Words: dined.branching.familiar

ACCESS:
Car park on the B3357 between Merrivale and Tavistock (What3Words: developer.drift.guesswork). From the car park cross the road and head south-west for about half a mile to reach the stone wall from where you can view Vixen Tor. From here you can walk a clockwise circle taking in Heckwood Tor, Pew Tor, the quarry pool and the Bullseye stone. From the Vixen Tor viewing point, follow the wall south to Heckwood Tor. From here it's a short walk south-west to Pew Tor (with a short diversion south if you wish to visit the quarry pool). From Pew Tor you then head north to the Bullseye Stone, and from there it's a short walk north-east back to the car.

Pillar, Heckwood Tor

Bullseye stone

Feather and tare marks

KES TOR

'The tor is a cohesive mass with a fine-grained core and a coarse-grained cap containing many rock basins, including the largest on Dartmoor...An inclusion of ultra fine-grained rock occurs on the south side of the tor, and the fine-grained core is exposed by a fall of rock from the west face. ...the antiquities clearly visible include the Longstone and stone rows on Shoveldown and Scorhill Stone Circle...It is not surprising that this convenient, level-topped viewpoint has long been the traditional grandstand for the Mid-Devon point-to-point races, the finishing post being just below the tor'.

Eric Hemery, *High Dartmoor,* 1983

It was on a visit to Kes Tor, many years ago, that we first explored Dartmoor's prehistoric remains. There are stone rows, a standing stone and one of the moor's most famous stone circles, Scorhill, all within easy reach of the tor, which is, itself, not far from the nearest road. There is also the famous Tolmen Stone, a naturally holed rock in the North Teign River. If you want to discover some Bronze Age archaeology and don't want to walk too far, this is a great place to start.

We have visited the tor and its surroundings many times over the years, always consulting our 'bible', *High Dartmoor* by Eric Hemery, to learn more about the local archaeology, history, and sociology. In the 1950s he lived in Chagford and Gidleigh with his then-wife Val and ran guided walks and pony treks. It was much later that he wrote the book for which he is now famous, which was published in 1983, and which runs to over 1000 pages, covering every aspect of Dartmoor, organised by its rivers.

His legacy lives on in his granddaughter, Emma Cunis, who runs walks and nature connection experiences on the moor, under the name Dartmoor's Daughter. She is a passionate advocate for the moor, and is very knowledgeable about it; she also believes it has a sacred, transformative dimension. We went to meet her at Kes Tor on a dull August day, as mists were descending round the tor. We were hoping it would clear up but weren't very confident, even in mid-summer. On Dartmoor they say that the tors can tell the weather – if you can't see the tors then it's raining, if you can see the tors then it's about to rain.

Following a warning from Emma about giving cows and their calves a wide berth, we hiked up towards the tor. Emma remarked on the prevalence of the *Molinia caerulea* – or purple moor grass – which was growing everywhere. When she was a girl there were far bigger patches of heather and gorse in this area, but now they're much smaller, as the purple moor grass takes over. This whole area is deeply intimate to her. 'We go back generations here on my mother's side. My mum grew up in Chagford and Gidleigh, so although we lived in Mid-Devon, we used to come here a lot: to Kes Tor and Scorhill and also Belstone. It was like our playground, in particular, Kes Tor, we used to scramble up and down it and hide in the rocks.'

Rock basin, Kes Tor

The cathedral-dome-sized cap of Kes Tor loomed up before us, and we sat down on its eastern side, to shelter from the strong wind. Emma described reconnecting with the tors as an adult. She had worked in London and around the world, but started to suffer from ME/Chronic Fatigue Syndrome and Fibromyalgia, and made regular visits back to Dartmoor to try and get better. She realised, through listening to her grandmother's stories, that her family connection with this part of Devon was key to her future well-being and a new career as a guide. 'I feel very strongly that we are sons and daughters of the land, we are not imposed on top of the landscape; I feel Dartmoor is a part of me. In my work, I want to invite people into a deeper experience of Dartmoor in a way that inspires them to care about it a bit more.'

We clambered onto the top of Kes Tor and found its famous rock basin, the largest intact one on Dartmoor at around 2 metres wide and 75 cm deep, created over thousands of years by repeated freezing and thawing of ice, chipping away at the granite, a crystal at a time. There used to be railings around it to stop sheep falling in, and you can still see the marks where the railings were fixed to the granite. Emma pointed out a small hole in a nearby boulder, dubbed the Kes Tor 'Eye', and also some letters, or a numeral- XI - marked in the stone above it, which she noticed a few years ago. She thinks it might be a tinner's mark, a watchful eye made to denote the boundary of a valued claim.

Sitting on the top, we could see a standing stone, called the Long Stone, with a double stone row leading north away from it to an unusual and intricate fourfold stone circle, in turn spawning its own double row. This area, to the south-west of the tor, is known as Shovel Down, and contains many rows, cairns and also a large ruined stone circle; it was obviously an important ceremonial site. Closer to the tor were hut circles, the remains of Bronze Age round houses. Then Emma told us about an interesting theory shared with her by an archaeologist: that there are the remains of a cairn around Kes Tor itself. There are a few of these 'tor cairns' on Dartmoor, where our Bronze Age ancestors built monuments around natural outcrops. These include Ugborough Beacon, Rippon Tor and Corndon Tor, but Kes Tor is not generally thought to be one of them. Yet when we looked around the bottom of the tor, we could see piles of stones that did indeed look like those from a cairn. This adds weight to the idea that ancient peoples saw the tors as a significant place in their cosmology. Emma told us: 'As I've grown older, I have thought a lot more about these natural features and how they might have been considered sacred, special, important. Obviously, we will never really know, but certain facts, such as the discovery of an ancient beaker at the Dewerstone, and the position of ritual monuments in relation to the tors, suggest this, as well as the way we ourselves relate to them now.'

Rival Tor
Crebear Pound
Berrydown
Scorhill Down
Wallabrook
SCORHILL CIRCLE
Watern Tor
Bridges
River Teign(N)
Tolmen
Balworthy
Round and Square Pound
Aboriginal Settlement
Teigncombe Common
River Teign(N)
Shuffle Down
STONE AVENUES
Triple Circle
Kestor
Cairn
STONE AVENUE
The Longstone (Menhir)
Holes made by former stones
Horse Hill
Three Boys
(REMAINS of CROMLECH)
Thornworthy Tor
Long Ridge
Bridge
Shepherd's Cottage
Kistvaen
Metherill Hut circles
FERNWORTHY CIRCLE
Fernworthy
River Teign S
Scale 3 inches = 1 Mile
Siddaford Tor
Logan
GREY WETHERS
ANTIQUITIES
BETWEEN
THE NORTH AND SOUTH TEIGN
The faint dotted lines indicate supposed line of Avenue when complete.

Leaving the tor, we made our way south-west to the Long Stone. There is a legend, common to many other megaliths across Britain, that the Long Stone can move by itself: that at sunrise it slowly rotates in its socket to warm each cold granite face in the sun. The movement of stones and men (or stones standing in for men and vice versa) certainly seems to be a key idea in reading these monuments.

From the Long Stone, we followed the double stone rows north. In Victorian times they were interpreted as passageways or processional avenues leading pagans to sacred places. Samuel Rowe, in his *Perambulation of Dartmoor* (1856) calls them 'parallelithons'. John Lloyd Warden Page, in *An Exploration of Dartmoor and its Antiquities* (1889) has this description of them, as seen from the top of Kes Tor. 'But what are those ranks of little men drawn up on Shuffle Down beyond the corner of Batworthy Wall? They are not men at all… nothing more or less are they than the remains of those parallelitha which once, in all probability, stretched northward to Gidleigh Circle and southward to Fernworthy Circle – a long two miles. Of this alignment and its contributaries but a small part is now left, but this is of so interesting a nature that we shall at once hasten down the slope of the tor in order to make a closer inspection.' There is a stunning engraving in the book, reproduced here, showing the rows in relation to the stone circles (see page 125).

We crossed the North Teign via the clapper bridge and walked a short distance downstream to visit the Tolmen Stone. Folklore says that if you can pass through it, you will be cured of rheumatism or other bone-related complaints. This stems from the idea of sympathetic magic– as stones look like bones they can heal them. The same idea means that the stone is also thought to have powers to make women fertile, the hole in the stone representing the womb. You have to be quite fit to benefit from it though, as the boulder is in the river and quite awkward to access. Our sons used to enjoy disappearing behind it and then popping up through the hole.

Retracing our steps to the clapper it was a short walk north to find the Scorhill (pronounced Scorrill) Stone Circle. Slightly marred by old cart tracks driven straight through the middle, it is an atmospheric, impressive place with some very large stones. Ruth E St Leger Gordon, in *The Witchcraft and Folklore of Dartmoor* (1965) relates a rather brutal tale about it which was told to her by an elderly man from Chagford in the second half of the twentieth century. 'Faithless wives and fickle maidens', according to him, were forced to wash in Cranmere Pool, run 3 times around Scorhill Circle, then head for the Tolmen Stone and pass through it, before finally running to the stone circles at Grey Wethers to kneel before the stones and pray for forgiveness. Any who the gods considered unworthy of forgiveness would be crushed by a falling stone. The old chap finished with a chuckle – 'that's why them's all fell over'.

Later in the book, St Leger Gordon also talks about horses refusing to enter the circle at Scorhill, and speculates that perhaps this is because of their sensitivity to the smell of blood. Perhaps rough justice, even ritual sacrifice took place here in the past? More recently, an issue of Dartmoor News magazine contained contemporary stories of horses and dogs being spooked, and even that of an adder who couldn't escape the ring, seeming to come up against an invisible barrier each time it moved towards the stones. Eventually, someone used a trekking pole to lift it and place it outside the circle where it slithered away into Gallaven Mire.

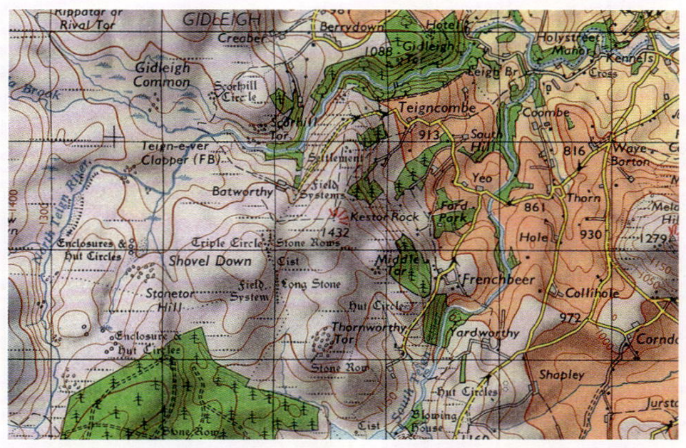

Double stone row

Tolmen stone

The Long Stone

KES TOR:
50.6608, -3.8895, SX 66545 86276
What3Words: surpassed.slogans.task

ALSO OF INTEREST:
The Long Stone and stone row: 50.6553, -3.8966, SX 66025 85678 What3Words: rinse.spruced.wealth
Scorhill Stone Circle: 50.6706, -3.9053, SX 65453 87397 What3Words: cars.stapled.stilted
Tolmen Stone: 50.6678, -3.9043, SX 65520 87087, What3Words: clotting.split.surcharge

ACCESS:
There is a small parking area near Batworthy Corner (What3Words: improvise.drop.eager) about 2.5 miles from Chagford. From here walk south-east to Kes Tor (about 10 mins' walk). If you want to visit the Long Stone and the stone rows, follow the path to the south-west of the tor, which takes you to the Long Stone. The stone rows lead directly north from it. To visit Scorhill Stone Circle and the Tolmen Stone, head north-west from the end of the stone rows, and cross the river over the clapper bridge. The Tolmen Stone can be found a short distance downstream; the stone circle is directly north of the clapper bridge.

SITTAFORD TOR

'On Sittaford Tor near here is a logan, and the tor is noticeable as being nearly the only one on the Moor clothed with verdure; sheep were browsing on its very summit on the occasion of my visit.'

John Chudleigh, *Devonshire Antiquities,* 1893

Sittaford Tor sits in quiet eminence at the gateway to the northern moor; the views from it are stunning: the high rolling grasses of Whitehorse Hill, the sweet black streams of Teign and East Dart, and the lush central Dartmoor basin towards Postbridge, seemingly threatened by a tsunami of dark pines emerging over the crest of White Ridge. But what really makes it special are the precious Bronze Age megalithic treasures that radiate from it.

Below the tor to the east is a rare double stone circle, Grey Wethers ('wethers' are castrated rams – the stones look like a flock of sheep from a misty distance). And just to the south-west is one of the most exciting archaeological discoveries on Dartmoor for many years: the Sittaford Stone Circle. This part of Dartmoor is a good example of one of those places where you feel our Bronze Age ancestors were intensely attuned to the landscape's unique forms, as well as to the particular nature and power of the stone, when creating their special ritual places.

It's never a quick walk to get there, given the tor's position deep into the flank of the moor; but it is straightforward from Postbridge or Fernworthy Forest; the latter is a slightly shorter walk so that is the option we chose on a moist, cloudy July day. We crunched up the foresters' grey gravel track, surrounded by the crowded darkness of the pines which somehow drained the place of life. Relief was provided by numerous colourful wild flowers beside the track, determinedly thriving in the margins: yellow tormentil and hawkbit, pale blue sheep's-bit scabious, and magenta and purple self-heal.

After about half a mile we came to the Froggymead Stone Circle and its associated monuments, standing in what Jeremy Butler (*Dartmoor Atlas of Antiquities*, 1991) describes as 'the middle of a miserable little clearing grudgingly allotted them by the Forestry Commission.' This place is richly textured with a stone circle, single and double stone rows and cairn circles; Historic England describes it as one of 'the most complete prehistoric ritual complexes on Dartmoor'. And yet the whole thing is hemmed in by industrial forestry. Although the forest was first created when there was an urgent need for wood during the First World War it was described by Jeremy Butler as 'the greatest single disaster to befall the archaeology of the moor,' because of the destruction of archaeological remains by the planting and felling.

We were glad to get out of the forest. What a contrast it was, away from all those trees: light and open, seeing each breeze's progress as it rippled across the sea of grasses. We could see the soft

Illustration from *Dartmoor A Descriptive Poem* by N T Carrington (1826)

Grey Wethers stone circles

peak of Sittaford Tor in the distance and began the gradual ascent up its slopes, cresting its shoulder to greet one of the most unusual ancient monuments on Dartmoor: the Grey Wethers double stone circle.

These two circles – each about 33 metres in diameter - stand together, virtually touching. The stones are notably large and rectangular, block-like, leading some to speculate that perhaps they were hand-dressed. But R Hansford Worth, in *Worth's Dartmoor* (1967) says there is no evidence for this, pointing out that the shape is due to the natural jointing of the granite, and that similar stones are to be found among the clitter on the slopes of nearby Sittaford Tor. This does raise an interesting question: was it simply too great an expenditure of effort to shape the stones or was it important that the stone was left undressed, a wild, naked rock more powerful and empowering?

All but three of the stones had fallen over the millennia but were re-erected by the Dartmoor Exploration Committee in 1909 and now, standing, have a seductive presence. Interestingly, there is a drawing of them by P H Rogers (reproduced opposite) which was published in 1826 in *Dartmoor: A Descriptive Poem* by N T Carrington. This shows them all standing, so he must have used a little artistic licence, as, in 1826, according to notes in the book by W Burt, around half had fallen at that time.

Walking among the stones, the angles constantly change, and the whole creation seems to move, stones crossing each other, weaving in and out of view. The Dartmoor Exploration Committee found evidence of large fires in the centre of the circles so we could imagine the stone's black shadows in the flickering orange light making the stones dance as well. The circles, never-ending, also speak to our idea of perpetual movement and eternity, just like the long-lived crystalline granite that they are made of. The fact that there are two of them perhaps speaks to something more animal; the instinct to couple and to perpetuate life.

Outlier stone, Grey Wethers

R J King, in *The Forest of Dartmoor and Its Borders* (1856) writes: 'In this gloomy district, even at midday, the circle of grey stones has a strange power over the imagination; but when the twilight is gradually closing, and the only sound that breaks the silence of the hills is that of the stream on whose banks they stand, the circles assume their ancient power.'

We left the circles and headed up the hill to the tor. Unusually, it incorporates newtake stone walls which farmers built in the 19th century, using the

tor as a natural barrier. There are also new barbed wire fences along one side and a couple of stiles, subjecting the tor to strange domestication amidst the wildness of its setting. There is a small grassy plateau at the top, where we stood admiring the magnificent views all around. There used to be a functioning logan stone here, but it disappeared in 1956. We could find no trace of it.

From the tor we followed the remains of an old wall, now a rubble vein in the mire, to the southwest for a short distance to find the Sittaford Stone Circle, which was discovered in April 2007 by Alan Endacott; the first such discovery on Dartmoor in a century. Gravity, time and building without any packing stones, mean they are now recumbent, but no less impressive for that (although there is one outlier that is still standing). The circle's diameter is pretty much exactly the same as Grey Wethers' nearby.

Alan, a self-taught archaeologist from a farming family born and bred on Dartmoor, has been studying and thinking about the Bronze Age monuments here since the early 70s. He was carrying out fieldwork in the area, as he had a theory there might be a stone circle there. Fortunately for him, there had recently been a huge wildfire: 'The ground was blackened and the turf scorched enough in places to reveal glimpses of the surfaces of several evenly spaced buried stones so I was quite excited on the day I discovered it. I went back a couple of days later to record it properly and probed the ground for further stones on the same arc.'

Alan informed Dartmoor National Park of his discovery and eventually, in 2015, the turf was removed from the stones, and the circle was revealed. The following year, in 2016, three of the stones were excavated. Pieces of carbon retrieved from beneath two of them were dated to around 2000 BC and subsequent samples to 1500 and 800 BC, giving dates by which those stones must have fallen.

Alan also had a theory that the builders of the circle positioned it in relation to Sittaford Tor, and in particular, the point at which the sun rises behind the tor on the Summer Solstice. On visiting it on June 21st, this theory was borne out. He added: 'It was a revelation to witness the Midsummer sun rising behind Sittaford Tor as predicted and imagining the impression this would have made on late Neolithic observers standing on the same spot.'

For Alan, the discovery was thrilling, not just because he had found a previously unknown circle. It also confirmed his theory of an arc of stone

Recumbent stones, Sittaford stone circle

circles, forming a chain around the central high ground of the Moor. He told us: 'The discovery, along with other stone circles I have recorded, bore out my theory that the arc of stone circles was continued beyond Grey Wethers and the White Moor circle to the north.' Alan's research suggests the tantalising prospect that this arc could even be part of an unprecedented mega-circle, a circle of circles that would have a circumference of about 22 kilometres, centred on Watern Combe.

As we stood looking over the circle, we felt grateful to Alan and his work uncovering this antiquity, and it made us wonder how many more are out there, hidden by thousands of years of decaying vegetation and peat growing inch by inch. We also reflected on whether the same builders were also responsible for Grey Wethers, so close by, and the others in the arc, part of some local chief or priest's megalithic masterplan executed over decades or centuries.

We walked the circle's circumference, looking at every stone bleached from their centuries-old bath in acidic peaty water. The ground was very boggy, and some of the orthostats were completely submerged under water, making small rectangular ponds that mirrored the skies above, making magical voids in the earth, watery graves for the standing stones. Crowds of delicate white bog cotton, like lambs' tails, were everywhere in the waterlogged ground.

Reluctantly, we left the circle to walk back over Sittaford Tor, and down over the tiny North Teign River to Teignhead Farm. This ruin was once a substantial complex with numerous buildings. John Lloyd Warden Page in *An Exploration of Dartmoor and its Antiquities* (1889), describes calling there for bread and milk to fortify himself during his hike. 'It is a wild place, and the bareheaded children – and there are always a small tribe in and around a Dartmoor cottage – see so little of man that, after a prolonged stare at the stranger, they bolt into the house like scared rabbits…An indescribable odour of peat-smoke and cream greets the nostrils, a curious but not unpleasant combination, because the door stands wide open, and the fresh Moor air which is driving the clouds so merrily across Sittaford Tor keeps all things pure and fresh.'

We left the farm, armed with a large stick to fend off a frisky herd of cattle and calves who were grazing nearby. Fortunately, despite a few aggressive bellows, they left us alone. We crossed a clapper bridge over the North Teign, disappearing back into the dark stands of Fernworthy Forest.

Froggymead stone circle

INFORMATION

SITTAFORD TOR:
50.6310, -3.9340, SX 63313 83044
What3Words: balanced.resolves.whirlpool

ALSO OF INTEREST:
Grey Wethers Stone Circles: 50.6320, -3.9261 SX 63876 83140 What3Words: relieves.heeding.trek
Sittaford Recumbent Stone Circle: 50.6287, -3.9381 SX 63014 82801 What3Words: flaunting.cheer.fidgeting
Froggymead Stone Circle: 50.6411, -3.90381, SX 65480 84119, What3Words: early.distilled.inner
Teign Head Farm: 50.6428, -3.9316 SX 63518 84349 What3Words: actor.annotated.dragging

ACCESS:
You can park in various places along the perimeter road at Fernworthy Reservoir; the best spot is on its south-western side (What3Words: eminent.cupboards.increment). From here it is a walk of about 3 miles to reach the tor. From the parking place, follow the road north-east for a short distance until it ends in a turning circle. Turn left here and follow the forest track. After 0.5 mile you will pass the Froggymead Stone Circle in a clearing on the right. Continue on the track for another mile until you reach the edge of the forest. From here walk south on the open moor to Grey Wethers, and from there head directly west to Sittaford Tor. The Sittaford Stone Circle can be found about 400 metres to the south-west of the tor, by following a stone wall.

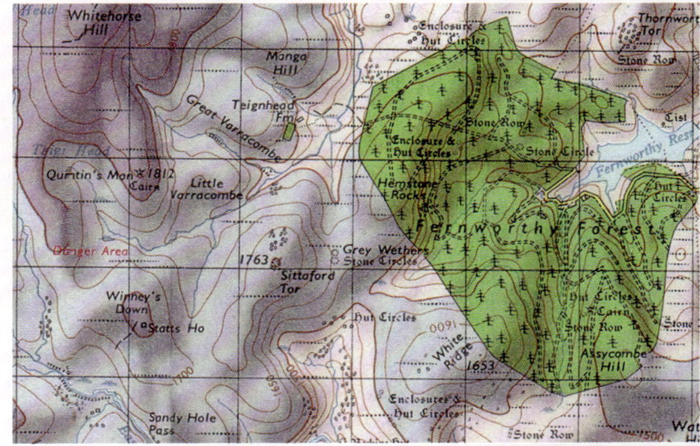

Teignhead Farm

Sheeps-bit scabious

Clapper bridge over the River Teign

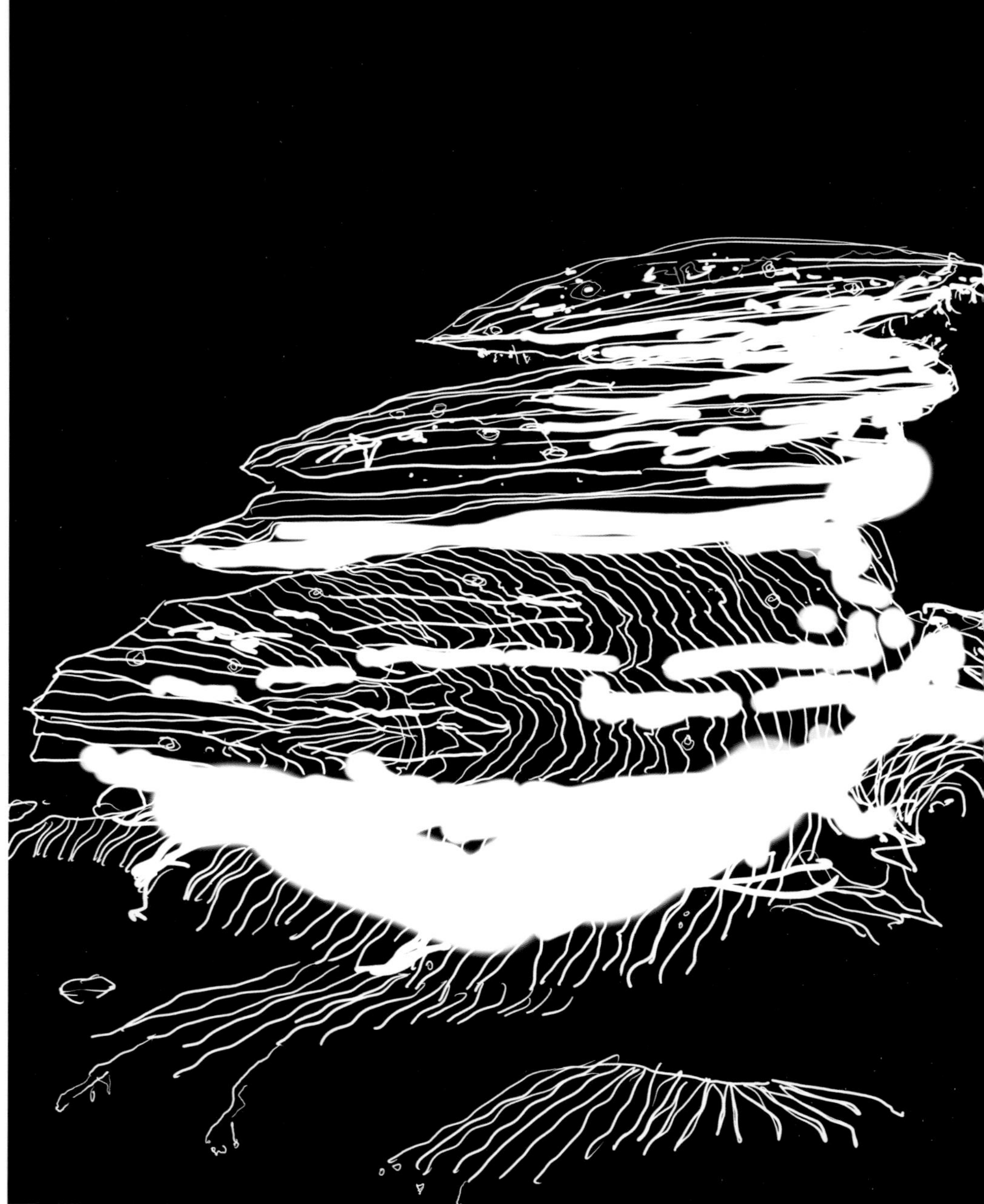

DEVIL'S TOR

'The view of the northern wilds from this lonely place includes the tops of Hare and Great Links Tors, Broad Amicombe, Hangingstone and Cut Hills (beyond Rough Tor) and Vur Tor, all rising above the sea of fen that stretches for five miles to Ockment Hill. A little to the south of Devil's Tor the fen ceases, and a rock, unnamed, far more shapely and significant than Devil's Tor proper – poised as it is on the brow of the ridge – affords a fine prospect of the Central Basin and the tors cresting Beardown ridge'.

Eric Hemery, *High Dartmoor,* 1983

Devil's Tor stands in remote country on top of a sodden plateau that drains great volumes of clear peaty water into the Cowsic and the West Dart rivers on either side. Right next to it is the solitary presence of Beardown Man, the second biggest standing stone on Dartmoor. It's hard to find a stranger or more haunting place. The tor is diminutive and no one seems to know the reason for its name but there is undoubtedly an otherworldly atmosphere here, with an incipient sense of sadness: ancient rocks surrounded by a sea of mires, a landscape that continuously weeps. And as Beardown Man points heavenwards – and maybe hellwards – one cannot help but think of human fragility and mortality.

We started walking from Holming Beam, a large car park beside dark pines, with a drab military hut. A small compound with a tall wire fence surrounded the hut; it contained a portaloo and empty dog kennels, as well as a green metal cupboard with FIRE BEATERS written on the doors in red. The army has been using Dartmoor for training since the early 1800s; in 1943 this area was used by American troops preparing for D-Day. There was a so-called 'target railway' in the valley below, where soldiers fired at moving marks which were hauled by cables along a sunken trackway.

Although it was the middle of August, with full sun predicted, heavy mist surrounded us, moisture which seemed to seep into every pore. We followed the track down to the tiny Cowsic river, where we crossed over a wooden clam bridge. The terrain immediately started to get boggy, and we hopped our way through a sea of purple moor grass, benefitting from occasional small pavements of stones laid across the wettest bits. Red and white poles drifted in and out of view in the gloom, indicating the boundary of the current military firing range.

We joined the Lych Way, an old track between Bellever and Lydford, known variously as the Corpse Road and the Way of the Dead. In the Middle Ages, this was the route to the parish church in Lydford on the western edge of the moor, the only sanctified graveyard for miles around where folk from Dartmoor had to be buried if they wanted to be saved. One can only imagine how tough it would have been wheeling the coffin in a cart from the centre of the moor for many miles across this inhospitable landscape. The mourners would have processed below Lydford Tor, where

Beardown Man

we decided to stop and wait for the dense white fog to dissipate before crossing the trackless mires to Devil's Tor.

The approach was strewn with large boulders, and also many flat stones set into the earth like enormous paving slabs. There was a strong wind, and we hunkered down under the largest crag which loomed above us, its side packed with horizontal jointings. In front of us were two small outcrops facing each other, nearly touching, which looked as though they were kissing. We ate some cheese sandwiches and decided to have a little snooze, in the hope that the mist would clear before the next stage of the journey which involved crossing a large boggy area with no path.

As we lay there, it felt surprisingly warm, and the breeze fluttered pleasantly across our faces, its power neutralised by the protective rocks above us. Drifting in and out of consciousness, we felt our bodies melding to the earth and stone below, and a sensation of being pulled deep down into the very heart of Dartmoor and all that it holds, unseen. We imagined the travellers on the Lych Way many hundreds of years earlier, taking shelter here and also resting in the embrace of the tor.

The mist refused to lift, so after about forty minutes, we set off again, still unable to see further than about 100 metres. A welcome highlight at our feet, luminous in the dimness, was a patch of British soldier lichen, *Cladonia floerkeana*, with its scarlet tips. It has a dark side though and, given our journey, we couldn't help remembering that another another name for it is 'devil's matchsticks'.

Then, finally, the wind started to blow a little harder, and, as if some god had switched the lights on, the landscape around us started to emerge through gaps in the mist. We glimpsed the other side of the Cowsic valley, a smooth green hillside studded with rocks, then the squat outline of Conies Down Tor above. We felt joyful and exhilarated by the views rushing past, with their colour and detail; liberated from the incessant grey gloom, and reassured by being able to see some of our surroundings.

Passing a group of large mounds made by tinners, we arrived at some unnamed rock piles which formed a long ledge. This small tor was one of the most elegant we have seen on the moor, a series of thin stacked discs gently tilted, a swirling vortex of the ever-present wind made solid. Covered in lichens, one of them had also a cow pat on it with mushrooms growing out of it, *Psilocybe cubensis*, known for its psychedelic properties. We speculated about the rock-climbing cow that must have eaten the mushrooms in the first place and managed to deposit this offering on a ledge halfway up a small tor. We knew we were nearing our destination, as this pile of rocks is about 250 metres south of Devil's Tor and Beardown Man.

As the deadening fog cleared, a different sense of isolation took hold as we started to see the wide

Small tor south of Devil's Tor

Dreaming at Lydford Tor

expanse of moor we had emerged onto. The rocky peaks of distant tors appeared: Fur Tor with its tower, Rough Tor with its military observer's hut, and Beardown Tors and Great Mis Tor to the south-west. We could see Beardown Man ahead for the first time, silent, still and solid. To its side was Devil's Tor, small and flat, like a sacrificial altar. As we approached, the ground got even spongier underfoot, with different types of sphagnum moss: some red and some green. This moss, which can hold copious amounts of water in its cell walls, was gathered on Dartmoor in the First World War for use as dressings in the trenches. As we approached the standing stone from the south, it looked like a substantial monolithic block, but as we walked around it, it transformed itself into a slim, ephemeral blade.

It is thought the stone would have been erected here about four thousand years ago, during the Bronze Age. It stands alone, unlike most of Dartmoor's other ritual monuments, which tend to have cairns and or stone rows/circles nearby. The name Beardown Man seems appropriate, as the stone does feel like a being, a kind of ancient version of sculptor Anthony Gormley's blank-faced iron figures, both confronting and contemplating the landscape. Gormley actually points out that the old megaliths are 'the ur-gesture of sculpture', one of the original sculptural actions taken by humans many thousands of years ago, who selected a stone and made it upright.

In fact, the word man, in this context, comes from the Celtic word maen, meaning stone. Sabine Baring-Gould visited it in May 1888 and reported his findings to the Devonshire Association in a report called Some Devon Monoliths which was published later the same year. 'It is, to my mind, the finest menhir on the Moor; the utter solitude and weirdness of the situation, and the bold character of the stone itself, and its sombre, sable vesture, make it impressive to the imagination. It stands above the present ground-line 10 feet 9 inches; but the ground about it is soft, boggy peat, and I was able to sink a rod 3 feet below, and feel the stone to that depth.' Interestingly, 'sable vesture' here refers to black lichen which he observed on the menhir, but there was none there on our visit. Perhaps atmospheric conditions have changed in the last hundred years.

Although Devil's Tor seems to be the lesser presence, being dwarfed by Beardown Man, maybe it is actually the father, and the standing stone its demonic offspring. Baring-Gould believed the menhir was a slab taken from the tor. Seeing them together is an affirmation of the power of stone both natural and man-made.

As the clouds raced past Beardown Man, against ever-changing skies, we paid homage to this stone that has been standing here for thousands of years, in all weathers. At least 120 generations of humans have stood in its shadow, although on this day we hadn't seen a soul for the entire walk.

Beardown Man

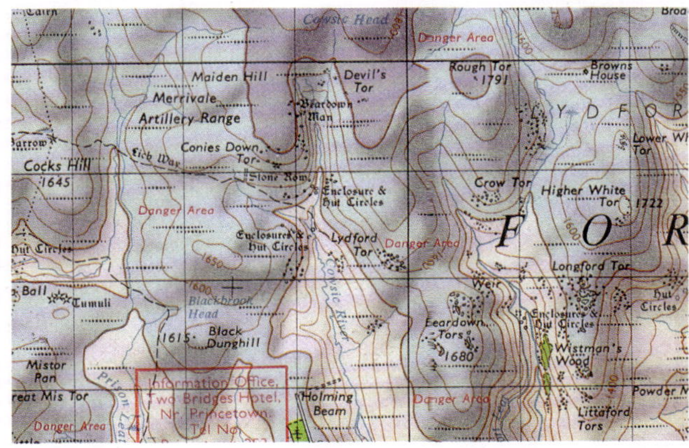

DEVIL'S TOR:
50.5994, -3.9845, SX 59645 79626,
What3Words: closet.pods.special

ALSO OF INTEREST:
Beardown Man standing stone: 50.5994, -3.9850, SX 59609 79630, What3Words: circus.usages.gifted
Lydford Tor: 50.5862, -3.9803, SX 59903 78150, What3Words: stupidly.composer.pound
Paddling pool in the Cowsic: 50.5767, -3.9863, SX 59452 77113, What3Words: skate.store.novelist

ACCESS:
The tor is situated within the Merrivale Range; check there is no firing before you go: www.gov.uk/government/publications/dartmoor-firing-programme. You will need an Ordnance Survey map and some navigation skills to get to Devil's Tor. It's about 6 miles there and back. It is also boggy, so do not attempt to visit after wet weather. Park at Holming Beam by the military hut (What3Words: expiring.curve.regularly).
Walk north-west along the track for a third of a mile and then turn right, still following the track, down to the river where there is a footbridge. Cross here and then head north-east to Lydford Tor (about 0.7 mile from the footbridge). From here walk north for about another mile to reach Devil's Tor.

'Kissing' stones, Lydford Tor

Psilocybe cubensis

LEATHER TOR

'...the fine form of Lether Tor, like a sentinel, guards the pass, faced by the great hill of Sheepstor, changing its hue every moment as the shadows cast by the clouds drift across its slopes. All along this part of the Moor the views are of extreme beauty, verging, indeed, upon grandeur... There are those who maintain that the most mountainous outline upon Dartmoor is that possessed by Great Mis Tor. But these cannot know Lether Tor. Although in altitude considerably less than the immense hill above the Walkham, this precipitous hill is in contour far more a true mountain.'

John Lloyd Warden Page, *An Exploration of Dartmoor and Its Antiquities,* 1889

The ancient Celtic tribe who inhabited Dartmoor and Devon were called the Dumnoni, a name thought to be derived from old Celtic 'dubno' which can be translated as the 'deep world'; fitting for a land of plunging valleys and high moors. Leather Tor is a place where this deep world emerges into the here and now. The tor stands proud like a forgotten Celtic queen, wearing robes of heather, looking down over river valleys winding to the seas. Three lesser tors stand next to her in a line, her warrior bodyguards, and small, conical fir trees dot the slopes below her like loyal retainers. An elegant peak with a surprisingly sharp spine, she is wild and imperious.

The valley below was quite heavily populated by Celtic and Bronze Age peoples in the years before the Romans. There were several villages of thatched round houses in the area, which remain today as groups of hut circles. The area is rich in their ritual monuments, including cairns, kistvaens and stone rows. There is also rare evidence of the Roman presence on Dartmoor along the main trans-moor road from Plymouth to Moretonhampstead. In 1863 a small hoard of Roman coins was found hidden under some boulders near Black Tor a little further up the road, perhaps left there for safekeeping by a passing legionary or merchant, worried about the local Celtic tribes.

The most spectacular view of Leather Tor is from the south-east, from Down Tor. It's an aspect that's been painted by many artists over the years from Victorian times to the present day, entranced by the sublime qualities of this stone rampart ('Leather' is probably derived from the Celtic word 'ledr' which means slope or cliff). However, the clitter-covered slopes make the approach difficult and we decided to walk down to it along the Sharpitor ridge from the trans-moor road.

Immediately we came across an unprepossessing but intriguing site, a double stone row right by the road next to Goad's Stone Pond where we parked. There is a theory that this pond is one of around 40 'sacred pools' on Dartmoor which would have been of both practical and spiritual use to our ancestors. Many of these have ritual and domestic prehistoric structures next to them, like the stone rows here, and artefacts have been found in them, suggesting they were important places. For example, some late Bronze Age spearheads were found at the bottom of one of the possible sacred pools, Bloody Pool near South Brent. And generally, across Britain and Europe we have seen that precious objects like axe heads, foods like honey and meat, and even slaughtered human bodies were placed as offerings in rivers, lakes and ponds at this period, showing that water was associated with other, sacred worlds.

The stone rows were quite hard to make out. The stones were small and scattered, many were buried, and the two kists at the ends were little more than rocky splashes. We did, however, with the aid of a plan of the site, manage to find the blocking stone which would have marked the end of the row. However, it was rather difficult trying to imagine how the row would have originally looked, while cars and vans rattled along the road next to us. The row's location is probably the reason it is so incomplete; it has been in a prime position for plundering by highway workers for centuries.

Our disappointment at the incomplete nature of the row got us wondering whether this ruination actually matters. Is knowing the row was there enough, and our imagination can do the rest, or would it be better if all these monuments survived intact? Perhaps they should be resurrected and reconstructed as the Victorian antiquarians did. Or are we too precious with our past? Are the remaining relics just another shallow human scratch on an ancient stone skin that should be left to heal? It is extraordinary that so many of them have survived at all, so we think whether patched and mended, feral and scattered, it is important that we remember the stones and the stones will remember us.

Leather Tor is part of a group of mountainous-looking crags around Burrator Reservoir, and forms part of a leisure playground for generations of Plymouthians who come here to walk, cycle and eat ice cream. The city lies just a few miles to the south, and the reservoir serving it was created in 1898 after sixty years of wrangling about the best location. A large area was flooded, resulting in the drowning of several working farms and many archaeological remains. As penance, South West Water, which now owns the site, is responsible for managing 25 surviving monuments which remain.

Leaving the road, Sharpitor, a chaotic pile of rocks, stood between us and Leather Tor. We hiked towards it, following a little stream which had its source in a spring at the tor's foot. Before heading on to Leather Tor, we took a short diversion to the south-west towards Peek Hill. On the way, we passed a small granite stone with the words DPA on it. These letters refer to the Dartmoor Preservation Association, which owns this area of land. It was founded in 1883, as 'a response to the impact of industrial scale mining, military encroachment and diminishing historic rights to access land.'

The story behind the DPA's purchase of this area is an interesting one, because it illustrates the political battles that have raged on Dartmoor for well over a century, between those who want to build and those who want to keep the moor free of human interference, or as the DPA puts it, 'disfigurement'.

It's hard to imagine now, but during the Second World War, this rugged part of Dartmoor was the site of a military base called RAF Sharpitor. Although hardly any traces remain, there was a host of buildings including barracks, a transmission tower, and workshops. After the war the site continued to operate, eventually closing in 1970. There was then an attempt to build a reform school here, presumably because the applicants thought it

would be a suitably tough environment for recalcitrant boys. The DPA, led by Lady Sylvia Sayer, successfully campaigned against the idea, and then later, in 1984, bought the land to preserve it.

There is one relic of this period that is still visible: the remains of a Cold War bunker constructed in 1957. The Sharpitor ROC (Royal Observer Corps) post was one of over 1500 built around the country, to be used for monitoring the effects of a nuclear attack. Devonport, the biggest naval base in Western Europe, is just a few miles away, and it would have been a prime target. Each bunker was designed to house three members of the ROC (known as the 'eyes and ears' of the RAF), with special equipment to gauge the effect of any nuclear blast.

Today, all that remains is a mound with a couple of stone hatches, but it is fascinating to wonder how much of the original bunker remains below ground. Not to mention what it would have been like, in the event of a nuclear blast, to be watching it all from here, and to be the only survivors, hunkered down in a bunker on Dartmoor in the aftermath of a nuclear apocalypse. It seems part of the perverseness of nuclear war logic that Dartmoor, seen normally as a tough and inhospitable, even a dangerous place to live, should be thought of as a place of refuge and shelter. It just shows how the landscape and its meaning to us will keep changing.

We retraced our steps to Sharpitor and picked our way through a large area of clitter towards Leather Tor. An overhang of rock at its foot looked like a little shelter. From this approach, it looked like a dragon's back rising from the bracken around it; over to the right, we could see the mountainous mass of Burrator. We climbed up its fractured granite spine, taking care as the drops on either side of us became ever steeper; this tor is one of those that gets frequently visited by Dartmoor Search and Rescue. Lots of flowers and other vegetation were growing amongst the rocks: heather, tormentil, and two small rowan trees, the mountain ash, peppered with acid orange berries.

We could see three much smaller, blocky stacks over to the south of the main pile. They are really all part of the same formation as the main tor, but some call this area Lower Leather Tor, which does make sense as it feels as though it has a separate identity. The three stacks all stand on one huge, shattered piece of granite which forms a kind of pavement or, at one point, staircase between them. These bodyguards keep watch over the dark waters below and Plymouth in the distance.

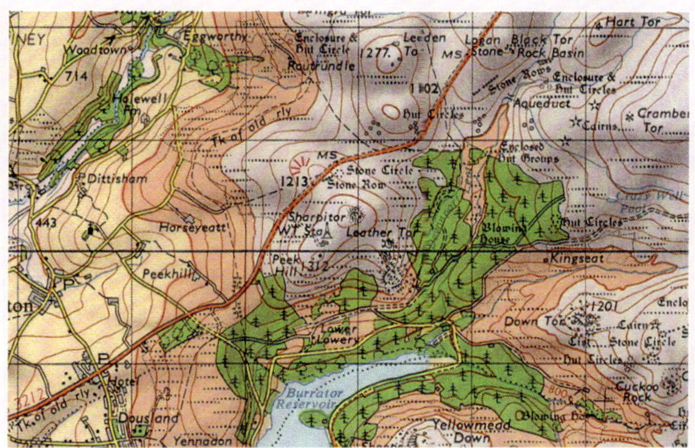

LEATHER TOR:
50.5121, -4.0286, SX 56263 70000, What3Words: combining.victor. whistling

ALSO OF INTEREST:
Sharpitor: 50.5149, -4.0327
SX 55976 70321 What3Words: spades.fruitcake.communal
Cold War ROC post: 50.5117, -4.0372, SX 55652 69976
What3Words: romance.quoted. bloomers
Lower Leather Tor: 50.5098, -4.0279, SX 56305 69752, What3Words: cyclones.dwelled.circular

ACCESS:
Park on the B3212 between Princetown and Yelverton, there is a parking area just by Sharpitor (What3Words: degree.canoe.below). From the car park walk south-east to Sharpitor. If you wish to see the Cold War bunker, follow the path south-west from Sharpitor for about 400 metres to find it. Retrace your steps to Sharpitor and then follow the path south-east through the clitter to find Leather Tor. (it's about half a mile from the car park without the detour to the bunker)

Lower Leather Tor

Remains of nuclear bunker

RIPPON TOR

'Rippon Tor consists of a number of scattered piles of rocks, though none of them are striking. But the visitor will, nevertheless, be well rewarded for making the ascent, for besides the magnificent view the spot is full of interest. Here the dwellers in the huts that stud the slopes in the vicinity of the hill brought their honoured dead for burial (as they did to other elevated situations on the moor) and in here in a later day, but one remote from us, the stone-hewer came to fashion the symbol of Christianity.'

William Crossing, *Crossing's Dartmoor,* 1912

The highest point for miles around, Rippon Tor is a shrine to the dead that is full of life and light, with its canopy of ever-changing skies, full of wind, sun, cloud and rain. The tor granite has acted like a magnet for memories for the longest time and there are cairns on it and around it; places where our ancestors, thousands of years ago, laid their loved ones and bid them goodbye for the last time. Standing on top, you can see how the cairns and the tor line up. In one direction they point to the sea where the luminous white stone of the Isle of Portland appears in the far blue distance on a clear day. In the other, they look into the high heart of the moor. Up here you feel part of something airy and indefinable. You can also see, from the top of the tor, the remains of the homes and working places of those who lived here in prehistoric times.

The tor is one of a handful on Dartmoor where Bronze Age people created cairns incorporating the tor itself. These uncommon monuments are called tor cairns. For them, the tors must have been places of significance and spiritual connection, and so the idea of enhancing the weathered natural rocks, dressing them, focusing in on them, seems logical. There is a large cairn around the highest outcrop: small loose stones are piled up on top of it, almost totally obscuring its peak. The cairn's apex has now been blunted, hollowed out for a trig point placed there by the Ordnance Survey who needed to reach the geology for a solid datum line.

There are the remains of another, smaller tor cairn nearby to the south-east. Stones are piled up around a distinct, twisted natural granite pillar. Then, a little further in the same direction, there are two more large cairns, loose rock piled up high, now hollowed and tumbling outwards from the efforts of the treasure hunters and stone looters.

Rippon Tor is very near our home and it's one of those places we've experienced in all weathers, and through different times in our lives, good and bad. Like the right sort of friend, it's been there through thick and thin, solid beneath our feet, always supporting us whether we realised it or not. On this particular visit, enjoying the warmth of a hazy summer sun, we decided to start by walking around the lower slopes of the tor, starting at Halshanger Common. The brutal buttressed brick structure of the 1940s rifle range loomed large and red across the other side of Rushlade Mire. With its rusting

Tor cairn, Rippon Tor

Unfinished cross

Edwardian visitors by the logan stone (courtesy Dartmoor Trust)

target winches and silted-up dugouts, it is now thankfully an anachronistic relic.

Passing a surprisingly tall hawthorn tree, (they are usually small and stooped) we arrived at a large hut circle that stands in isolation. When it was lived in it would have been a small thatched roundhouse, and is probably part of a settlement which is recorded on the Ordnance Survey map a little further to the east. The fact that this humble domestic dwelling is still here, four thousand years after it contained living, breathing beings, is remarkable. This area is known for its well-preserved Bronze Age farms. As well as hut circles there are the remains of old reaves (ancient stone boundaries) nearby. The Dartmoor reaves are evidence of a first wave of enclosing, or marking out, this land at a large scale, dating from around 1500 BC. Over 400km of these low walls of piled-up boulders run across the tops of major Dartmoor watersheds and reach down into the fertile valleys below, becoming petrified in modern field systems.

Following the contours around to the east, we arrived at a dry-stone wall, the great-grandchild of a reave, which leaned at a precarious angle, seemingly held up by little more than the breeze. From here there are the best views over Haytor and Saddle Tor, their enormous granite stone butts like sleeping giants. It was a short hike uphill alongside the wall to Rippon Tor, where we stood at the top to catch our breath.

The views were astonishing. We could see the Teign estuary, a silvery ribbon that glinted in the light, leading down to the sea at Teignmouth. Over to the north-west was the whale's back of Hameldown, and down below us, to the west, just on the other side of the road, we could see the outlines of Foale's Arrishes, a palimpsest, an over-written page, of human farming from prehistoric

Halshanger firing range

through medieval to Victorian times. The land at Foale's Arrishes was worked over thousands of years by different generations of farmers and there was even a pub there in the nineteenth century, serving thirsty miners as they passed on their way to the Stannary town of Ashburton. Today you can still see the remains of ancient stone walls which enclosed the land in small parcels, and at least eight hut circles. Charcoal, pottery and flint flakes were found during excavations at the site in 1896. Over the years, the settlement varied in size, but the one constant would have been Rippon Tor, a powerful presence watching over it.

We clambered over the stones that formed the tor cairn around the main outcrop, to the trig point in the middle. From here we could see the small but distinctive pillar of rock to the side that is the other tor cairn. There are small stones embedded around the bottom of it; the remains of a large pile of rocks that would have surrounded the pillar, making a striking monument with the natural stone column rising from the centre.

Not far away, hidden in a crevice in a small outcrop, was a small plastic box. Inside was a pad with a note saying it had been placed there in 2016 by Dartmoor Dave as part of the Seven Tor Challenge. The latest entry – a couple of weeks ago - was from seven-year-old Dylan, proudly writing that he'd just done his first-ever wild camp. He wasn't even born when the box was first placed there.

Two large cairns stood near the tor, surely placed there in relation to it. There are so many questions about these mysterious piles of stones. How big were they originally? Were they built at the same time? Which came first, the ones on and around the tor, or the ones standing a short distance away? If we dug them up, what might we find? Human ashes, or perhaps bones if the bodies were left for excarnation?

Returning to the tor, we walked around to its western side, where we found a large unfinished stone cross lying on the ground. Charles Spence Bate, one of the Victorian founders of the Devonshire Association, believed it to have been carved 'in situ' to ward off non-Christian spirits emanating from the pagan cairns nearby. However, later commentators, although agreeing it was carved where it lay, have suggested that it was originally intended to be moved to another destination, once it was finished. Although the cross and the cairns come from widely different religious traditions, their stone voices speak harmoniously of finding truth in the high places.

We left the tor and started the descent back to the car. On the way, we passed a smaller tor which is marked 'Nut Crackers' on the Ordnance Survey map. This is the site of one of Dartmoor's most popular logan stones in Victorian times. John Lloyd Warden Page in *An Exploration of Dartmoor and Its Antiquities* (1889) notes it as an attraction: 'On the side of the hill, and about a quarter of a mile to the south-west of the summit, stands an immense oblong logan… probably the largest within the moorland borders. It is poised on a perpendicular block of granite, and is in length sixteen feet by four in breadth and thickness, and may be moved by some effort by mounting up the extreme end and stamping steadily.'

That the stone was popular is evidenced in numerous old photographs of it from the late Victorian period, through to the 1960s/70s, in the archive of the Dartmoor Trust. There is one in particular, (see page 150) showing a party of solemn Edwardian visitors, standing by the balanced stone, dressed very formally in bonnets and boaters, and presided over by a dog-collared vicar. Amazingly, there still is a living link to the people in the picture. 90-year-old Wendy Major, who lives in nearby Ashburton, remembers the woman at the middle front, with the walking stick, who was called Mrs Simpson. Mrs Simpson was a schoolteacher who taught Wendy at the age of 5, in 1940.

Sadly, the stone is no longer there; it disappeared in the 1970s. Despite this being a relatively recent event, there is no reliable account of what happened. F H Starkey, in *Exploring Dartmoor* (1980) says it was 'blown up by vandals in 1975' but, infuriatingly, gives no more details. Some locals believe it was toppled deliberately by local soldiers, others say it fell off naturally. Another popular theory is that the logan stone fell victim to the sonic boom of Concorde which flew over regularly at the time.

In memory of the fallen stone and these enigmatic lithic lovers from the past, we thought we would recreate this image. On a late summer Sunday afternoon we rounded up some friends and hiked up there for a picnic and some photography. It was difficult to replicate the picture exactly; although we positioned our friends as precisely as possible, many of the massive stones on which they had to sit or stand seemed to have moved. There is always the feeling on Dartmoor that, despite appearances, nothing stays in the same place for very long.

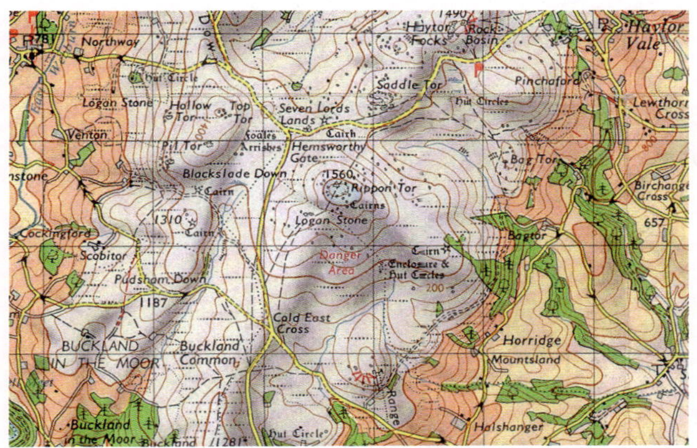

RIPPON TOR:
50.5664, -3.7716, SX 74626 75577, What3Words: error.spot.generated

ALSO OF INTEREST:
Cairns to the south east of the tor: 50.5657, -3.7703, SX 74715 75493, What3Words: propelled.ribcage.soils
The Nutcrackers: 50.5637, -3.7753, SX 74359 75278, What3Words: optimally.growl.breakfast
Foales Arrishes: 50.5686, -3.7829, SX 73829 75838, What3Words: kebab.commit.grading ;
Bronze Age hut circle: 50.5584, -3.7735, SX 74468 74696, What3Words: whirlpool.scenes.cloud

ACCESS:
Park at Cold East Cross (What3Words: kidney.edges.depths). Leave the car park from its northern side, cross the road, and go through the gate. It's a walk of about a mile north from here to reach Rippon Tor, passing the Nutcrackers on your left. Alternatively you can park at Hemsworthy Gate (What3Words: vets.stiletto.shun) and follow the path south-east up to Rippon Tor.

View to the RIver Teign

BRAT TOR

'Above us on the R is Bra Tor, or which is a fine cross, about 13 feet in height, erected by the late Mr W Widgery, the well-known artist, in commemoration of the Jubilee of Queen Victoria in 1887. Unlike the ancient crosses of the moor this one is not hewn from a single stone, but is composed of a number of blocks. Seen from any point this cross seems perfectly in place, but appears to the best advantage when viewed from the valley of the Lyd, below the confluence of that stream with the Doe Tor Brook.'

William Crossing, *Guide to Dartmoor,* 1912

Brat Tor looms over the north-western edge of Dartmoor, with views over North Devon and Bodmin Moor in Cornwall. A large stone cross sits on top of it, a testament to Dartmoor's transformation, in Victorian times, from a grim place to be feared, to a romantic region worthy of exploration and artistic appreciation. The cross was placed there by William Widgery, one of Dartmoor's most famous artists. Entirely self-taught, he was born in 1826 in North Devon and trained as a mason. He moved to Exeter and started painting in his spare time, before turning professional, and producing thousands of pictures in watercolours, oils and print. His images of dramatic landscapes, with enhanced light and colour, show that artists like himself, influenced by others like J M W Turner, were changing perceptions of wild landscapes from 'barren wastes' to places of romance and sublime beauty.

It's generally accepted that Widgery was quite happy to indulge in a bit of artistic licence in his compositions to achieve the appropriate drama. On one occasion, a passer-by, looking at the work-in-progress, noticed there was a river in the foreground of the picture, which wasn't there in reality. 'Mr Widgery', he said, 'there is no river at the foot of that hill.' 'Isn't there?' returned Widgery, without looking up. 'Well, there ought to be.'

The nineteenth century, when Widgery was operating, saw Dartmoor opening up to visitors. The Industrial Revolution had resulted in people having more leisure time, and the advent of train travel meant they could get around the country more easily. Tourists started to arrive, clutching illustrated guidebooks, and news of Dartmoor started to spread. William grew increasingly successful and his son Frederick, often known as 'F J', continued the family business, going to art school and also becoming a painter.

William built himself a house at Lydford. (It still stands, and is now a hotel). He lived there for around ten years, and no doubt frequently walked up Brat Tor, which is probably what gave him the idea of placing a cross there to commemorate Queen Victoria's Golden Jubilee. Well over a century later, the cross is still standing and is visible for miles around.

We visited it one blustery September day, as the bracken was starting to turn brown at the edges, and the leaves on the trees were losing their brightness. It was a gradual ascent of a mile up to the tor; we crossed the River Lyd via some stepping stones and said hello to a group of adults with learning disabilities who were on their way down. As we neared the top, the shaft of the cross gradually disappeared from view, until the entire thing was invisible. We walked around the southern edge of the tor, picking our way over huge fallen slices of stone, one of which had an enormous low overhang.

Approaching the top from the south-eastern side, there were more fields of clitter to navigate, but also stunning views of the graceful peaks of Chat Tor and Hare Tor in the distance, and the central basin of the moor beyond. Three red flags were flying, indicating army manoeuvres in the neighbouring Willsworthy Range. One was on the ridge next to Chat Tor, another on Hare Tor, and another on Sharp Tor, a little nearer to us.

We could now see the cross ahead and walked through large and small piles of horizontally jointed grey granite to reach it. This side was far rockier than our initial approach from the west. We climbed up and reached the cross on top of the tor where, bizarrely, we saw a squirrel clinging to the top. Frightened by our dog, it had fled up there to safety, and just as quickly, disappeared. We speculated on how on earth it had ended up here; the nearest wood is some way away.

More in keeping with the Victorian Gothic nature of the scene, a pair of glossy blue-black ravens circled as we climbed down the western side to view the cross from a different angle. It stood upon an imposing granite cliff. It would have been quite a feat to have erected it in such a windswept place, and it's a tribute to Victorian building skills that it's still standing today.

Leaving the tor, we headed off east towards the Doe Tor Brook, picking our way through more fields of clitter, to find the remains of the Wheal Frederick Mine, or as it's also known, Foxhole Mine. Tin was extracted here in the mid-nineteenth century, about the same time as William Widgery was finding success as a painter; Dartmoor was still a hard-edged industrialised landscape even as the artists moved in to romanticise it. There are the remains of a large building with two intact fireplaces; this could have been the mine captain's residence, or the count house, from which the mine was managed (most likely both). There was once a leat here, where water was siphoned off from the brook, and a small tramway, as well as a wheelpit which we found just to the north of the main building, filled with stones. To the east of the

Widgery Cross

Raven's nest

Witches Pool

count house was the dressing floor, where there were two buddles, or circular pits, where the tin ore was separated from the rock.

Standing among the ruins, with no other humans in sight, the only sounds we could hear were the tinkling of the brook running along beside us and the croaking of the ravens flapping heavily above. How different an atmosphere there would have been here during the mine's heyday nearly two centuries ago. This small patch of Dartmoor would have been busy and noisy, with the sound of machinery pumping, fires roaring, the banter of the workers, and the screaming brakes of the trams.

Following the brook downstream, we passed an enchanting sequence of frothy waterfalls, mossy chutes and peat-brown pools. Small willow trees nodded over the water, two of them bearing large, messy raven's nests in their fragile branches. As the stream turned west, there was another, bigger waterfall, plunging into an infinity pool looking out over the valleys below, where we stopped for a quick swim. Moving away from the brook, we found a stone pillar with the words TRDC on it: Tavistock Rural District Council making their claim to the watershed. A short distance away, by the stream, was a square concrete box with a drain cover on top covering the leat that once siphoned off water for local consumption.

The final stop on our walk was Witch's Pool – also known as Hunter's Pool - on the River Lyd, back on the western side of Brat Tor. This is a famed wild swimming spot, a large round pool under a commanding cliff called Black Rock where there is a plaque in memory of Captain Nigel Hunter, who was killed in action in France in 1918. It was placed there by his grieving parents in the year after he died. In 2008, on the 90th anniversary of his death, the original plaque, which was becoming

Foxhole Mine

worn and illegible, was replaced with the one that is there today.

It is a very moving memorial, containing an extract from a poem called Widgery Cross that he wrote in 1915 while on a visit to Dartmoor, on leave from the hell of the trenches. His diary describes a busy weekend, playing golf with his father in Okehampton, followed by lunch with his family. On the Friday evening, he went for a walk with his dog Gyp along the Lyd and Brat Tor, on the Saturday he played tennis and on the Sunday he composed the poem after attending church. It is a poignant account of saying goodbye to Dartmoor, with the implicit awareness that he may never return. He compares human life to 'this moorland stream', where 'the dark still pool is the end of all.'

'Are we not like this moorland stream
Springing none knows where from,
Tinkling, bubbling, flashing a gleam
Back at the sun; e'er long,
Gloomy and dull. Under a cloud;
Then rushing on again…'

BRAT TOR:
50.6514, -4.0672, SX 53956 85574, What3Words: bachelor.filer.culminate

ALSO OF INTEREST:
Witches' Pool: 50.6497, -4.0769, SX 53262 85399, What3Words: carbon.collides.shatters
Ruined mine house: 50.6498, -4.0584, SX 54574 85377, What3Words: admire.openings.chosen
Small 'infinity' pool in the Doe Tor Brook: 50.6478, -4.0669, SX 53969 85166, What3Words: vase.community.unions

ACCESS:
There's a car park near the Dartmoor Inn on the A386 (What3Words: stunner.craftsmen.confronts). From here follow the track north east for about half a mile until you reach the stepping stones and the bridge over the River Lyd. Cross the river and continue for another half a mile east to the top of Brat Tor. To find the mine ruins, walk south-east of the tor for another half a mile to find the ruins by the Doe Tor Brook. You can finish the walk by following the course of the brook west back towards the car park; then pick up the River Lyd in a northerly direction where you will find Witches' Pool.

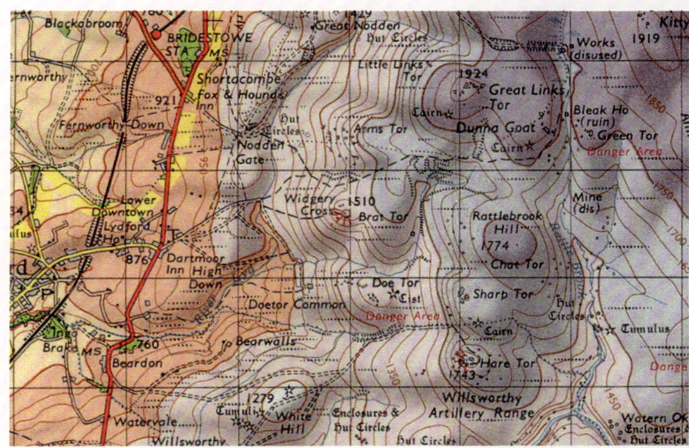

Maidenhair Spleenwort

Doe Tor Brook

WHITE TOR

'As we mount the slope towards White Tor…we shall notice the vallum surrounding the pile, and which renders it one of the most curious tors on the moor. Several of the rock masses are incorporated into this rude wall which, on the E side, is in a better state of preservation than elsewhere. Remains of hut foundations occur within it, and a number of flint chips have been found among these, and around the tor. This circumvallation differs from the ordinary hut pounds, and seems to have been constructed for defensive purposes.'

William Crossing, *Guide to Dartmoor,* 1912

White Tor is a jagged, broken enigma. It is not white, it is steely grey, nearly black as, unlike most tors, it is not made of granite but of dolerite, a hard, dark grey sub-volcanic rock with a green tint of olivine, known locally as greenstone. It is the only tor on Dartmoor to have the word 'fort' in Gothic script next to it on the Ordnance Survey map but it is probably not a fort. It looks like a natural tor from a distance, but up close it is pimpled with mounds of small, lichen-covered stones, both natural and man-made, as well as the remains of two walls that were built around its summit thousands of years ago. We know ancient people created buildings and enclosures here, but there is no real agreement about the type of settlement it was.

It's a gradual uphill walk of about one and a half miles to reach the tor from Smeardon Down. On a changeable August morning, we filled our eyes and lungs with the crystal-clear views of the distant tors over to the south-west of us: Great Mis Tor Roos Tor, and finally Great Staple Tor, with its grand avenue between its two pinnacles. Stopping for a rest, we smelt that the greenstone on which we were sitting had a cushion of wild thyme, the small pinky-purple flowers bright amongst the aromatic green leaves.

Passing Boulter's Tor, a suspended cliff on the left, we found Stephen's Grave. This is a small stone monument by the track, a rudely fashioned block of stone with the letter S engraved into its plinth. Like Jay's Grave near Widecombe, this is a sad reminder of how people who took their own lives were treated in the past as sinners: buried without a funeral, in unhallowed ground at a crossroads, even with a stake through the heart. The story of this grave goes back to the late eighteenth century, when a local man, John Stephens, poisoned himself after his heart was broken. It's not known when the memorial was placed there, but the plinth was erected in 1936, by the Dartmoor Preservation Association.

From Stephen's Grave, we could see the clear outline of a pound on the slopes of White Tor: a large circle of stones for livestock, enclosing the remains of a Bronze Age village. Up ahead, the needle rocks of the tor pointed skywards. We climbed towards it, stepping over a large area of grassy hummocks, some covered with gorse. These

Kistvaen and thufurs

are called thufurs, dating back to the Ice Age, and were formed millions of years ago by patches of ground freezing and then thawing. They are more commonly found in Iceland.

As the leaden peaks of the tor grew nearer, we could see vast piles of loose, much smaller rocks surrounding them. The summit of White Tor is encircled by two massive concentric ruinous walls of the same small stones. At the centre, we could see a large cairn enclosing a pointed, natural piece of rock, a structure we now knew was a tor cairn like those we'd seen at Ugborough Beacon and Rippon Tor. To the side, there was another taller stack, with a dagger edge. A large flagpole protruded from one of the rocks.

The walls at White Tor create what's known as a 'tor enclosure', a type of ancient structure only found in South West England, and dating back to the early Neolithic period, between five and four thousand years BC. What makes these places distinctive is that they surround and incorporate natural rock formations in their construction. There is obviously a practical reason for doing this – keeping livestock in and keeping enemies and predators out (like at Grimspound or Dewerstone). However, here at White Tor there is no evidence of habitation when the walls were built; the hut circles and stores found inside the walls came a long time afterwards. This would make this place more like a henge, an enclosing ceremonial, spiritual space like stone circles.

This idea is reinforced by the tor cairns where boulders have been piled around natural stone outcrops, emphasising and acclaiming the presence of these monoliths erupting out of the ground by singling them out. Even more than on the other tors, because there are several of these tor cairns and the site is so particularly stony, there is the sense that the tors were significant in their own right as part these spiritual places; sharing their longevity, whispering their stories of the underground world.

Maybe the tors had spiritual significance to the ancients here in the same way as stones and other natural forms did to other peoples around the world. In the South Pacific, the cracks and fissures of volcanoes were seen as the ancestors' entry and exit routes to the earthly realm. In Australia 10,000

or cairns on White Tor

The Langstone Menhir

years ago, the great isolated mounds of Uluru and Kata Tjuta became places of the ancestors and the earth rising up in grief at the death of men. Closer to home in Scandinavia, each family of the ancient Saami had their own hallowed hill upon which the rock formations were the most sacred of places.

White Tor was excavated by the Dartmoor Exploration Committee in 1899, who found pieces of pottery, flint and charcoal, and who recorded the walls, tor cairns and hut circles. The flints showed the site had been in use 10,000 years ago in the Mesolithic, soon after the last Ice Age. At this time and into the Neolithic, Dartmoor would have been wooded, and White Tor would have been the exception to this rule: a kind of roof light out onto the wider world, with views out across the moor and to the lowlands beyond. Even more than now the tor would have felt like a kind of liminal space between the earth and the sky.

We took our time to wander around, exploring the rocks and admiring their fantastical shapes, split and pointed. The rock is dolerite, not granite. Like granite, it was once molten magma and has similar qualities to basalt. But because it occurs in smaller volumes it cooled faster, and so the mineral crystals are much smaller and hard to see with the naked eye. Dolerite rocks contain a larger proportion of olivine crystals than normal, giving the stone a green hue. Dartmoor geographer Sharon Gedye suggests this greenstone at White Tor may have been seen as sacred by our ancestors, because of the unusual colour. Elsewhere across the UK and Europe in the Neolithic, greenstone was celebrated in the form of highly valued ceremonial greenstone axe heads.

Many of the rocks now have a dappled appearance, being covered in lichens of white, grey and black, including one that looks like tiny grey eruptions from a volcano, hence its name *Stereocaulon vesuvianum*. A poetic echo of how this tor was formed underground millions of years ago.

On previous trips to the tor we have also visited the Langstone Menhir, just half a mile to the east, and the Langstone Moor stone circle, another half a mile on from the standing stone to its south-west. Both of these later-period Neolithic monuments are very much worth seeing. They were reset upright by the Dartmoor Exploration Committee in the late Victorian period but were vandalised by American troops stationed here during the Second World War. The soldiers fired bullets and shells at them for target practice, and in the case of the circle, knocked down and blew up many of these ancient stones, leaving fractured remains.

INFORMATION

WHITE TOR:
50.5898, -4.0607, SX 54228 78711
What3Words: disgraced.various.
sharpened

ALSO OF INTEREST:
The Langstone Menhir: 50.5903, -4.0494, SX 55024 78739
What3Words: hairstyle.perplexed.
ballots
Langstone Moor Stone Circle:
50.5856, -4.0406 SX 55636 78198
What3Words: durations.draw.transmits
Stephen's Grave: 50.5844, -4.0694, SX 53592 78122 What3Words: fidget.
fluffed.proper

ACCESS:
There is a car park at Smeardon Down (What3Words: fabric.pack.blinks). From here it is a walk of 1.5 miles to the tor. From the car park, follow the lane east for a short way and then fork left up a track. After a mile you pass Stephen's Grave on the right, and then the tor is shortly after, up on the left. The Long Stone is a walk of half a mile directly east from White Tor. To find the Langstone Moor Stone Circle circle, you need to follow the path south west from the standing stone, for half a mile. NB (The Long Stone and the Langstone Moor Stone Circle are in the Merrivale Range so check firing times before you go; White Tor is not in the range).

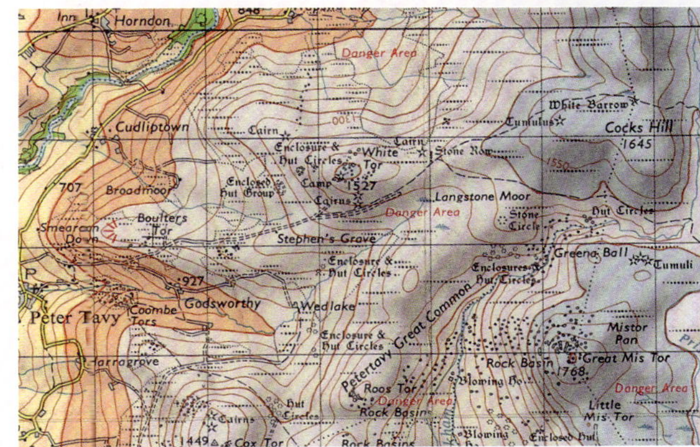

Langstone Moor stone circle

Snow Lichen 'Vesuvius'

White Rim Lichen

FUR TOR

'This Tor must always be the favourite of the moorland initiate. Every obstacle an unqualified impatience can discover encircles it. It is the central throne of a region which winter cannot mar, nor summer touch, with transforming magic... Enislanded in passive decay and soundless desolation, everything repels; there is not even the relief of sullen resistance; every line and curve is acquiescent in fate, for peat is the least strenuous product of dissolution imaginable.'

T A Falcon, *Dartmoor Illustrated,* 1900

William Crossing memorably described Fur Tor as a 'wilderness of stone'. It is the most isolated and inaccessible tor on Dartmoor, in the middle of an enormous mire created by the headwaters of River Tavy to the west and the River Dart to the east, as well as their myriad streams. Getting to it is never easy, and it is not a walk for the faint-hearted. There are many routes, whose pros and cons are the subject of passionate debate. Because of this, it has acquired something of a legendary status, and is often referred to as the 'Queen of the Moor'.

There is undeniably something special about this 'wilderness of stone'. It is an isolated, eerie world where stones erupt in wild abandon, from under a skin of blanket bog. Our ancestors must have felt something of this, and on Cut Hill, just to the east of Fur Tor, there have been two phenomenal discoveries which have recently been revealed after thousands of years below the dark peat: a stone row and a kistvaen, built by Neolithic peoples. Work is still being done to assess and understand these findings, and work out how they relate to other archaeological remains on Dartmoor.

Early one September morning, during a brief Indian summer, we arrived through the high-hedged lanes at Baggator Gate, near Peter Tavy. Here we picked up the Lych Way, an old track which was used by moorland people for centuries to get to church at Lydford. We passed a military hut, marking the start of the Merrivale firing range, through which we were going to walk, to get to the Okehampton range, in which Fur Tor is located. Plans for any visit must involve checking firing times on all three ranges, as the routes go through them all. On the day of our expedition, there was firing at Willsworthy, hence our chosen route from Baggator, one of the less trodden routes to Fur Tor.

And so began a long, gradual ascent, which was to take three hours. Leaving Baggator behind, we could see the distinctive green disc of Round Wood (South Common Plantation) below us, its circular wall indicating perhaps an old cattle pound, now planted with trees. Then we turned north along what we thought would be a track but was actually a rocky gully or sunken way. In Victorian times this was a route – called Black Lane North - to a peat works at Walkham Head; pack ponies would have brought the peat down this track, for burning in the mines at nearby Mary Tavy. It was dug out to provide a flat surface for the ponies to walk along, but decades of erosion have resulted in its collapse.

Mires restoration project

For centuries, peat was an essential part of life on Dartmoor. It was used as fuel for cooking and heating and was also used to make turves, from which houses were constructed. Each family would have their own 'turf tie' where they would cut peat for their personal use. In the nineteenth century, there were attempts to extract it commercially, but none lasted long, as coal and eventually electricity triumphed.

As we strode further into the heart of the moor, we were grateful for the eroded trackway, which gave us something to follow in the increasingly smooth landscape. Bog stretched around us as far as the eye could see. The ground was becoming increasingly wet, and the track itself was getting more and more indistinct, so we were cheered to come across a small walker's cairn (apparently known as Ken's Cairn), from where we got our first sight of Fur Tor, which was still a very long way off. A short time after this, the track petered out completely into the mire. We knew we had to walk east to find the Tavy Valley, from where we would head down to its confluence with Fur Tor Brook, before climbing up to Fur Tor. At least the sun was out, meaning that wet feet wouldn't be a big issue.

It was a beautifully clear day, and soon we could see the River Tavy below us, a tiny thread of water at this stage of its early life. (A little further downstream it becomes wider, passing through the picturesque glen of Tavy Cleave, which is another, very scenic, route to Fur Tor). A kestrel hovered over us and small green frogs jumped out from beneath our feet as we descended through the glistening bogs towards the confluence where we could see large areas of flattened grasses, and rubber mats laid down on the approach to the river. It was obvious that heavy machinery was at work, and it was at that point that we noticed several large yellow diggers on a ridge over to the east of Fur Tor.

It was quite surreal seeing these hefty iron vehicles silhouetted on the ridge, like strange long-necked beasts, in the remotest part of Dartmoor. They are part of a multimillion-pound project to restore peat bogs here and on Exmoor and in Cornwall. Over centuries, the peat has degraded, in part due to human interference with the water table, and the aim is to re-wet it and block the places where water escapes. The idea is that this will allow the peat to store carbon and water more efficiently; it will also stop the flow of water off the moor, mitigating the impacts of climate change and helping to prevent flooding in towns and villages lower down.

These are undoubtedly laudable aims, but some people are worried about the impact of the machinery on the delicate moorland ecosystem, as well as its historic features. The Dartmoor Society has been quite public about its concern that not enough attention is being paid to the effect of the ground disturbance on the ancient archaeology in which Dartmoor is so rich. Its founder and former Archaeologist for Dartmoor National Park,

Dr Tom Greeves, has even described the project as 'pointless vandalism'.

We crossed the Tavy and started the ascent to Fur Tor, which appeared as two separate entities: on one side, an enormous slope strewn with clitter large and small, and, higher, and to the east, a more compact, taller pile, with a large chimney-like stack on top. Making our way through the rocks scattered on the tor's slopes, we stopped for a rest, and, to our delight, discovered a functioning logan stone. It made a gentle, deep subterranean knocking sound when rocked, a noise that travelled up through the bones to the heart. It also felt 'spongy' to push and was almost furry from its lichen covering; stone transformed into something soft and organic through having found this temporary point of balance. All in all, a small but seductive experience which made us feel sad that so many logan stones, such popular attractions in Victorian times, have been vandalised or otherwise succumbed to the march of time.

As we got to the top, we could see rocks of all shapes and sizes, muddled together in wild abandon. The main stack stands proud on the edge of a large ridge, where there are about five other stacks, an archipelago of stone. We found a ledge to sit on, warm in the sun, and had some tea, all the while taking in the views into Tavy Cleave, over to High Willhays and over the Tamar to Bodmin Moor and Brown Willy on the faint horizon. Small clouds now scudded low across the hills their black shadows skittering over the brown moorland beneath them.

It was odd though, having been promised isolation and freedom from other people at this 'remote' and 'lonely' spot that we could watch the workers on the peat restoration project digging nearby, whilst down in the valley we admired two

Sphagnum moss

shepherds on their quadbikes skilfully commanding their quicksilver collies to gather their flocks.

And then, as if to prove that loneliness is a state of mind, we were joined by three men, laden with enormous backpacks, who'd walked out from Postbridge. They were visitors from Portsmouth getting away from the bustle of the city. They love Dartmoor so much they visit it twice a month to camp for a night or two. They told us they usually avoid spending the night at Fur Tor because there's too much of a 'wild camping scene'.

Pixies are said to live at Fur Tor. There is an interesting theory that the reason for this legend is that after the Celts were pushed back into Cornwall by the Saxons a few remnants hid in remote places like this. As the Celts were supposed to be generally smaller in height than the Saxons the conquerors told stories of the 'little men' hiding in caves.

Over to the east, we could see Cut Hill, further and higher even than Fur Tor, a strange landscape dominated by peat hags, dark slashes in the ground. Sabine Baring Gould has a wonderful description of the hags in *A Book of*

Dartmoor (1900). 'In the depths of the moor the peat may be seen riven like floes of ice, and the rifts are sometimes twelve to fourteen feet deep, cut through black vegetable matter, the product of decay of plants through countless generations. If the bottom be sufficiently denuded it is seen to be white and smooth as a girl's shoulder – the kaolin that underlies all.' Peat, decaying plant matter, forms at around a millimetre a year so these hags would be at least 4000 years old. In other places on Dartmoor, the peat is over 7 metres thick.

Reaching Cut Hill, a short walk from Fur Tor, we were overwhelmed by the sheer weirdness of the place. Peat hags rose out of the ground around us, weeping wounds in the earth. A small cairn indicated the peak. Beyond this, we could see a large, coffin-shaped stone lying on the ground. It had a white luminosity, which comes when the quartz stones have recently been uncovered from the acidic peat and not had time to get covered in lichen. This is one end of a stone row, which was discovered by Tom Greeves in 2004 (of the Dartmoor Society, mentioned earlier). There is a line of 6 or more large flat slabs, which would originally have been upright. Unusually, they seem to have been set up with their thinnest profiles aligned along the axis, so they would have almost vanished when seen from the ends of the row.

This discovery caused huge excitement at the time, because until this point there had been no prehistoric finds in this area at all. Talking to the BBC in 2010, after the site had been excavated, Dr Greeves said: 'This has really changed our thinking about this part of Dartmoor. Literally nothing has been recorded, structure-wise, over a four-mile circular diameter until now…The interesting thing is the NE-SW orientation, so the midsummer sunrise is over the north-east axis and the midwinter

'Coffin stone' at Cut Hill stone row

Peat hags, Cut Hill

sunset is over the south-west axis. This is the same as Stonehenge, but these stones predate the ones at Stonehenge. So we know that prehistoric people had a sophisticated interest in midsummer and midwinter. And this is clearly a sacred hill.'

It's thought the stones were placed there in the fourth millennium BC, earlier than many of the other stone rows and circles on Dartmoor. And if this discovery were not exciting enough, a large kistvaen, possibly a double grave, was found there in 2021 by Paul Rendell, which it's thought may link to the stone row. He reported it to the authorities and the site was excavated in August 2024; two layers of wood were found inside, as well as what looked like fabric and some small round objects, possibly beads. This is rare, as organic matter usually rots away quickly underground - here it has been preserved in the oxygen-depleted peat. The remains of the kist have been taken away for further analysis; at the time of writing, results are awaited.

Standing by the row with these charismatic stones in their bed of black peat, we were alone but not alone. We gazed to the horizons, across the West Country and felt again a strong sense of connection to these people of the past, those walking Dartmoor now, and the land that connects us together across time.

INFORMATION

FUR TOR:
50.6300, -3.9986, SX 58744 83058,
What3Words: paces.implore.paused

ALSO OF INTEREST:
Cut Hill summit cairn: 50.6274,-3.9832, SX 59821 82739, What3Words: pelted.cooks.variation
Cut Hill stone row: 50.6276, -3.9825, SX 59872 82756, What3Words: essential.tripped.smaller
Logan stone: 50.6291, -4.0039, SX 58361 82966, What3Words: samplers.sliding.oppose

ACCESS:
There are many routes to Fur Tor, from north, south, east and west, all of them challenging. Around half the walk is through bog, so do not attempt it in wet weather or after heavy rain; take a map and compass; don't rely on your phone. You also need good visibility. Total walk distance there and back is a minimum of 8 miles. Military firing also needs to be taken into account: Fur Tor is the Okehampton firing range, and routes to it go through the Merrivale and Willsworthy ranges. Check firing times on www.gov.uk/government/publications/dartmoor-firing-programme. We walked from Baggator Gate, near Peter Tavy, where there is a small parking area (What3Words: trickling.wasps.retain). From here it is a 4-mile walk to Fur Tor (5 miles to Cut Hill). From the car park, follow the track east past Baggator on your left. Go through a gate where there is a large military hut and keep left along the stone wall. At the end of the wall head north along the track/gulley passing Lynch Tor on the right. Follow the gulley as it heads north-east and eventually peters out. From here continue north-east across the bog until you see the Tavy valley ahead of you. Walk north to cross the river at its confluence with Fur Tor Brook, and from here follow the range marker poles for a short distance east before heading north to Fur Tor. To get to Cut Hill (which is visible from Fur Tor), follow the path east from Fur Tor for another mile.

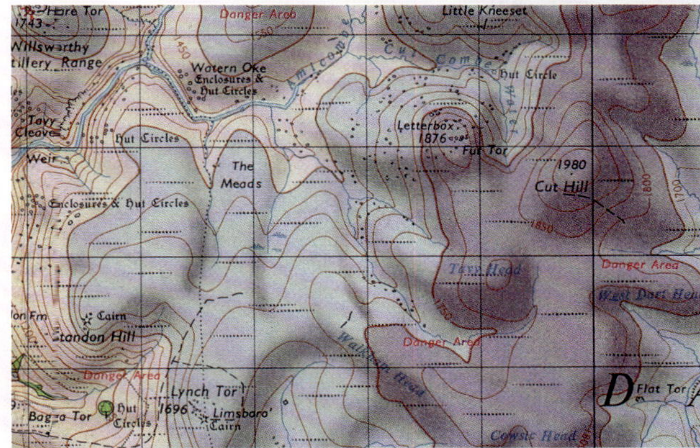

Logan stone south of Fur Tor

WATERN TOR

'This tor consists of three fine masses of rock – the southern resembling an immense cardinal's hat – and is geologically interesting as exhibiting, in an unusual manner, the intersection of lines of parting in granite. The northernmost piles approach so closely at the top as to present the appearance of but one crag, perforated by a large opening. This curious aperture is known as the Thirlstone (Anglo-Saxon thyrelan, to pierce), and is, indeed, referred to by this name in the Perambulation of 1240 and the Survey of 1609.'

John Lloyd Warden Page, *An Exploration of Dartmoor and its Antiquities,* 1889

Watern Tor is an ice-carved gothic masterpiece of whirlpool granite. With outlandish gaps, like a decayed set of teeth, it dominates the skyline above the equally gappy smile of the Scorhill stone circle, which sits in the valley below. Perhaps our ancestors, the early farmers who built the circle, felt inspired by the charismatic presence of the tor as a natural megalith. Standing inside it, looking towards the tor in the distance, you can feel there is a relationship between these two significant places of stone.

It's quite a hike to get to the tor, a walk of at least eight miles (there and back from the closest lane at Scorhill Farm). The first thing that greeted us was a sign on the moor gate, put up there by the Gidleigh Commoners Association, the contemporary farmers that use that area as common grazing for livestock. Although the word commons implies that anyone can graze their animals here, this has not been true since the Norman Conquest. Landlords, notably the Duchy of Cornwall, have always been in control of who has commons rights. Now they are given alongside the ownership or tenancy of certain farms or estates and there are currently around 850 registered commoners who are allowed to graze an allocated number of livestock 'units'.

The sign bore the headline FOR YOUR SAFETY PLEASE KEEP YOUR DISTANCE FROM ALL CATTLE ESPECIALLY COWS WITH CALVES. We weren't surprised, having heard about a particularly problematic herd roaming this part of the moor in recent months that had injured a runner.

We walked down to the stone circle at Scorhill, one of the best known on Dartmoor, probably because of its easy access, being close to the road. It had a luminous, vibrant quality in the golden early morning September sun; the light was soft and the shadows were long. The stones seemed to glow, and almost quiver. In the distance Watern Tor high on the horizon also shimmered, its distinctive jagged shapes discernible, despite the distance.

Mindful of the warning about livestock, we warily eyed a herd of black cattle that was grazing behind the circle but they showed no interest in us, so we headed on north-west. After about a mile we reached the Buttern Hill stone circle, smaller than Scorhill, now ruined. Three stones, one an unusual shape like the head of a bird, are

Scorhill Stone Circle

still standing, but the others are either lying on the ground or missing, stones that have gone feral. A report by R Hansford Worth for the Devonshire Association in 1932 (later published in the compilation of his work, *Worth's Dartmoor*) has a diagram of the circle in which the positions of the stones are recorded, along with the dimensions and other features. What is particularly interesting is that the plan includes an arrow from the centre of the circle indicating the direction of the Thirlestone at Watern Tor. Worth does not refer to this in the text, but clearly believed the circle was built in relation to the natural landmarks around it. In the same report, a plan of Scorhill Circle also has an arrow pointing to the Thirlestone, as well as to Kes Tor.

Both of these stone circles are part of a so-called 'sacred arc' of circles that form a crescent along the north-eastern side of the moor when plotted on the map. So they not only connected to the tors but also to each other in a complex and beautiful diadem of granite monuments. And some people think that there could actually be a 'circle of circles', made up of stone circles that are, as yet, undiscovered.

From the Buttern Hill circle, we continued walking east, entering into a land of uneven mounds which were made by people streaming for tin around Ruelake and Gallaven Brook. Up ahead we could see a solitary black cow fairly near the path, but decided to keep walking, largely because there was nowhere else to go. All seemed fine as we passed, and then, with no warning, the cow charged. We stood firm and started yelling and waving our walking sticks at it. It was terrifying. There was no cover we could retreat to that was safe. No trees, no scrub, no hedges, just open moorland covered with mire and ankle-twisting grass tussocks, ironically a landscape made by thousands of years of livestock grazing.

The cow stopped its advance and for a while there was a short standoff. We separated, Sophie walking on with our dog which seemed to be the main cause of the cow's agitation, and Alex continuing to face off the cow, which started tossing its head, another danger sign. Alex started to retreat, but the cow decided to pursue the dog, running around the side of the path, heading us off. Fortunately, it

Dinger Tor

and think. This is because Dartmoor's granite is tilted upwards to the north.

Reluctantly we left this mesmerising panorama and started walking north towards High Willhays. The ground was boggy and the path melted away from time to time. As we neared the most southerly stack, which was an attractive ziggurat shape, we could see a group of young people climbing up the side. We stopped and chatted to their teacher, who told us he was getting them acclimatised for Ten Tors – an annual hiking challenge organised by the Army, which takes place every May. Teams of teenagers complete a gruelling two-day expedition, including an overnight camp, where they have to navigate routes of 35, 45 or 55 miles, carrying everything they need. As the youngsters, laughing and joshing about, climbed off the tor and disappeared down the hill, their teacher confessed that part of the point of today's hike was 'to weed out the idiots'.

As the school party headed off in the direction of Dinger Tor, we approached the main outcrop which looked like a battleship: long, low and grey. Rather appropriately, it seemed to have a mast - a long fibreglass pole sticking up from behind the cairn on the summit. It turned out it actually was a mast – an aerial – which belonged to Omar Sadek who was sitting beside it, wearing headphones, on the other side of the cairn. He was broadcasting as part of a project called 'Summits on the Air', a scheme for amateur radio operators where they make contact with other radio hams and talk to each other from the top recognised summits.

Omar told us he became involved after a terrifying solo traverse, without a harness, across a mountain in Slovenia. 'It was at this moment when I wished I could speak to someone…anyone. There was no phone signal. I was there, alone with my

thoughts - so I thought about *who* I might want to send a postcard to and *what* I might write. This gave me some sense of security. Mountains vary, but once you reach a certain altitude, life becomes invisible. It's as if someone has drawn a perfect line, separating warmth from bleakness. Separating colour from sepia. It's beautiful, but it can also look and feel desolate up there.'

He added: 'Being an outdoor enthusiast, amateur radio adds a whole new dimension to where I choose to hike. The higher up you go, the better you can broadcast and receive. I love the challenge of getting up high, seeing who I can reach.' It's nice to know amateur radio is still alive and well, despite the prevalence of mobile phones. And it is still needed; Omar is a volunteer with Raynet, a national body of radio amateurs who provide communications in times of emergency and also during public events. Last year he volunteered at a mountain biking marathon on Exmoor, a location where mobile phone coverage is poor.

This place has attracted others who find different kinds of voices and energy in high places.

Unknown to the majority who visit, Yes Tor is one of the 19 holy mountains of the Aetherius Society, which was founded in the mid-1950's by George King, a London taxi driver and yogi. In the 1960s King, along with various disciples, came to Yes Tor and also Brown Willy on Bodmin Moor to channel cosmic energy into them. Members of this worldwide New Age religion believe that these mountains and other peaks across the world now contain a reservoir of spiritual energy which can be released for the good of the world through prayers said by pilgrims who visit the tor.

The idea of mountains and high places as holy and spiritual sites has an ancient history and is shared by religions and philosophies around the world. From the 10,000-year-old Neolithic standing stone cults in the Eilat Mountains of Israel, to the Shugendo mountain worshippers of Japan today, mountains have been venerated in their own right as deities and as places to be nearer to the gods in their heavens. In the British Isles, there have been holy mountains for thousands of years. In Ireland, at 764 metre-high Croagh Patrick in County Mayo, pilgrims still climb barefoot to a summit dedicated to St Patrick. Long before the Christians came, Bronze Age people built standing stone rows nearby that align with the sun as it appears to roll down the side of the mountain, and so, in Celtic times, Croagh Patrick was associated with the sun god Lugh.

Although worn and weathered, there are still signs that High Willhays has also been a spiritual place for many thousands of years. Five neolithic cairns span the ridge. Four of them would have been big mounds, including one covering a chambered tomb; all are likely to have had some sort of human burial or cremation at their centre. The fifth cairn is a rarer variant, a ring cairn.

Ring cairn, High Willhays

Right at the centre of the ridge, this ring cairn consists of a 20m wide circle of loose stones incorporating an arc of the natural granite outcrop. It is an empty space that seems to be more about defining a special site. It creates a raised circle that joins with the mountain granite on this highest point, generating a place to contemplate human life, stone and sky together. It seems important that the granite is included here as an equal partner in this ritual site. This connection with the stone is even more apparent nearby at the extraordinarily shaped tor of Branscombe's Loaf, visible high up across the West Okement Valley a mile as the crow flies from High Willhays. Here there is another ring cairn that has been built to encircle the tor completely, showing a people marking and honouring the living rock as a place of transition between worlds.

As we passed by the High Willhays ring cairn on our way to Yes Tor we could see that it was filled with a shallow pool of rainwater. In its centre we could see the pale yellow sun reflected in the black peat water, shimmering and flickering as the breeze made ripples across the surface.

INFORMATION

HIGH WILLHAYS:
50.6851, -4.0110, SX 58031 89204, What3Words: dome.tickles.stylists

ALSO OF INTEREST:
Yes Tor: 50.69365, -4.0106, SX 58087 90152, What3Words: rewarded.freezers.nails
Dinger Tor: 50.6753, -4.0020, SX 58636 88101, What3Words: charities.supply.chairing

ACCESS:
High Willhays is in the Okehampton Firing Range so check firing times on www.gov.uk/government/publications/dartmoor-firing-programme.
The nearest place to park is at the end of an unclassified road which leads onto the moor from Okehampton Camp. The parking spot is just to the south-west of Rowtor (What3Words: freedom.pitch.waged). The quickest way to get to the tor is to follow the track south from the parking place for about half a mile and then fork right to walk up to the ridge on which High Willhays stands (a walk of about 1.5 miles). For a longer and less steep walk you can follow the track from the car park south to Dinger Tor, from where it is another gradual climb north-west to High Willhays (this route is about 3 miles) From here you can walk north along the ridge to Yes Tor, and then north-east from there to West Mill Tor and back to the car.

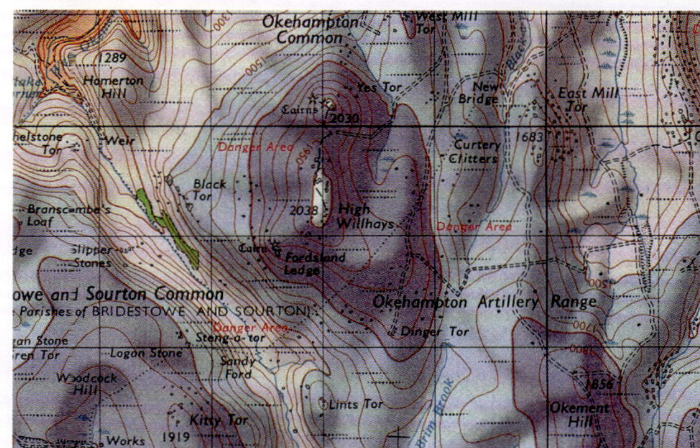

Yes Tor triangulation point

Army hut, Yes Tor

GLOSSARY

Barrow (burrow): An ancient burial place usually consisting of a mound of earth and/or stones, also known as a tumulus. They are usually known as cairns (ref) on Dartmoor, where they tend to consist of round piles of stones above the burial site. Some have pits which would have contained the ashes of the deceased person.

Beehive hut: A small stone building with a domed roof made by tinners in which to store their tools and ingots.

Blowing hut or house: A medieval building where tinners worked smelting ore and casting ingots.

Bury: An oval structure of stone and earth built by warreners to encourage rabbits to burrow into and breed. Also known as a pillow mound.

Cairn: A pile of stones: (1) A raised round, oval or long mound of stones over a burial place; some have a retaining circle of upright stones around them called a cairn circle (ref). Typically it would cover a kistvaen (ref) which might contain an internment of bones, ashes and other offerings like axe heads or jewellery.(2) A mound of stones made as a landmark eg for marking a boundary or made by travellers for wayfinding.

Cairn circle: A circle of upright stones surrounding a burial place, usually a kistvaen (ref). The upright stones would usually act as a retainers for a mound of stones and/or earth covering the kistvaen. These are smaller than stone circles (ref) and are often confused with them when the stone mound has disappeared over time, and the circle of stones remains. A well-known example of a cairn circle is the Nine Maidens stone circle near Belstone.

Cist: (also kist, kistvaen) See Kistvaen

Clam: A wooden footbridge.

Clapper: A stone bridge consisting of granite slabs on top of stone piers. The earliest are medieval.

Clitter (also clatter): scatterings of smaller rocks below a tor; they are the result of its fragmentation in earlier times.

Cromlech: see Dolmen.

Dolmen: (also cromlech) A type of above-ground burial chamber, where megaliths were erected, covered by a capstone. It was originally thought that these would have been covered in earth, to make a barrow, but more recently it has been thought that they were left as impressive stone monuments.

Excarnation: When the bodies of the dead are deliberately left out in the open so that the flesh is eaten by scavengers or rots away. This is so the bones can be collected and interred.

Gert: a deep, opencast working made by miners.

Gorge: a deep valley excavated by its river.

Growan: the Westcountry term for decomposed, weathered and crumbled granite before it disintegrates into china clay and mica sand.

Hut circle: The stone remains of a round thatched house from prehistoric times. They are usually found in groups, as people settled together in villages. The base of the hut would be a low stone wall, the top was made from wooden rafters, supported on central poles, covered with thatch or turf.

Kistvaen: (also kist, cist) A small burial chamber from the Bronze Age; the word is thought to be derived from the Celtic for 'large box or chest' (kist) and 'stone' ('maen', in Devon dialect 'vaen'). A square or rectangular pit was lined with granite slabs to make a box, into which the deceased person's body was laid in a contracted position. They were also used to inter bones or ashes which were sometimes placed in an urn or a beaker. A coverstone was placed on top. Many were then covered by a cairn.

Lake: A Dartmoor word for a small stream.
Leat: A man-made watercourse, designed to convey water by gravity from its point of diversion from a stream.
Logan stone: A rock which, through natural erosion, has come to rest in such a state that it can be 'logged' or rocked without falling off.
Maen: A Celtic (Cornish) word for a stone.
Megalith: Literally a 'big stone' the term refers to stones that make up many different forms of prehistoric monuments around the world.
Minilith: A term introduced to indicate that many prehistoric monuments use small stones to create circles, rows and geoglyphs (lines of stones that make shapes, for example spirals, animals or spirits).
Menhir: A tall standing stone from the prehistoric period (a Breton word derived from the same Celtic word root as the Cornish word maen).
Orthostat: A stone that has been placed upright.
Reave: An ancient land boundary made of earth and stones created in the Middle Bronze Age.
Rock basin: A naturally occurring hollow found on the top of tors.
Ring cairn: A man-made, ring shaped, mound of small to medium sized stones enclosing a space that may be empty, or have a separate central burial cairn, or natural rock outcrop, within it.
Stone circle: A ritual monument from the Bronze Age in which both large and small stones were set upright to form a circle. This was a space set aside for special activities, meetings, trade, or ceremony. They are often aligned on landscape features and celestial events like the rising and setting of the moon and the sun. Excavations on Dartmoor have revealed that fires were held inside some of them.
Stone row: Another ritual Bronze Age monument, in which stones stand in a line, usually in relation to a cairn or other burial place, and sometimes a menhir (ref) or blocking stone. There are single, double, triple, and multiple stone rows on Dartmoor. Like the circles, they were often aligned on landscape features, as well as the sun, moon and stars.
Tare and feather: A way of cutting granite. Holes were drilled along the line intended to be cut; wedges, the feathers, were placed around a central spike, the tare, in the line and then struck, to split the stone.
Tolmen: A large holed stone made either naturally or hollowed out by people as a megalith. There is a notable natural one on the North Teign near Scorhill stone circle.
Tor: A prominent rock outcrop; the majority on Dartmoor are of granite.
Tor cairn: A prehistoric ceremonial site comprising a mound of stones around, or covering the base of, a prominent natural outcrop of rock.
Tor enclosure: A large hilltop or hillslope enclosure in South West England, surrounding or incorporating natural rock outcrops, defined by one or more circuits of stone-built walls. All are prehistoric; some are definitely neolithic.

Reconstructed kistvaen, Lakehead Hill

BIBLIOGRAPHY AND WEBSITES

Baring-Gould, S, *A Book of Devon* (1899, Methuen, London)

Baring-Gould, S, *A Book of the West* Volume 1, Devon (1899, Methuen)

Baring-Gould, S, *A Book of Dartmoor* (1900, Methuen)

Breton, Revd H Hugh, *Beautiful Dartmoor and Its Interesting Antiquities* 1911 Hoyten and Cole, Plymouth)

Butler, Jeremy, *Dartmoor Atlas of Antiquities Volumes* 1-5, (1991-7, Devon Books in association with Halsgrove)

Carrington, N T, *Dartmoor: A Descriptive Poem* (1826, Hatchard, Piccadilly & R Williams, Devonport)

Chudleigh, John, *Devonshire Antiquities* (1893, Henry S Bland, J Townsend, Exeter)

Collingwood, Josephine, *Dartmoor Tors Compendium* (2017, Tavicinity Publishing)

Collingwood, Josephine, *Geology of Dartmoor* (2022, Tavicinity Publishing)

Cresswell, Beatrix F and Almy, P H W, *The Homeland Guide to Dartmoor* (1948, The Homeland Association)

Crossing, William, *Guide to Dartmoor* (1909, Western Morning News, Plymouth)

Crossing, William, *Gems in a Granite Setting* (1905, Western Morning News, Plymouth)

Crossing, William, *Amid Devonia's Alps* (1888, Simpkin Marshall)

Falcon, T A, *Dartmoor Illustrated* (1900, James G Commin, Exeter)

Harvey, L A and St Leger Gordon D, *Dartmoor* (1953, New Naturalist Series, Collins, London)

Hemery, Eric, *High Dartmoor: Land and People* (1983, Robert Hale, London)

Jones, Andy M, *Preserved in the Peat* (2016, Oxbow Books)

King, Richard John, *The Forest of Dartmoor, and its Borders* (1856, John Russell Smith, London)

Martin, E W, *Dartmoor* (1956, Robert Hale, London)

Newman, Phil, *The Field Archeology of Dartmoor* (2011, Historic England)

Norman, Mark, *The Folklore of Devon* (2023, University of Exeter Press)

Page, John Lloyd Warden, *An Exploration of Dartmoor and its Antiquities, with some Account of its Borders* (1889, Seely & Co, London)

Piper, Max, *East Dartmoor's Lesser-Known Tors and Rocks* (2022, The Dartmoor Company)

Petit, Paul, *Prehistoric Dartmoor* (1974, David and Charles, Newton Abbot)

Rendell, Paul, *Exploring around Burrator* (2007, The Dartmoor Company)

Richards, Colin and Cummings, Vicki, *Stone Circles A Field Guide* (2024, Yale University Press)

Rowe, Revd Samuel, *A Perambulation of the Antient and Royal Forest of Dartmoor* (1856, J B Rowe, Plymouth)

Smith, Vian, *Portrait of Dartmoor* (1966, Robert Hale)

Shrubsole, Guy, *Who Owns England?* (2019, William Collins)

Starkey, F H, *Exploring Dartmoor* (1980, F H Starkey)

St Leger-Gordon, Ruth E, *The Witchcraft and Folklore of Dartmoor* (1965, Robert Hale, London)

Walker, Jack, *Dartmoor Sun* (2005, Halsgrove)

Worth, R Hansford, *Dartmoor* (Papers edited by G M Spooner 1953, executors of the late R Hansford Worth, Plymouth)

WEBSITES

Legendary Dartmoor
www.legendarydartmoor.co.uk

Tors of Dartmoor
www.torsofdartmoor.co.uk

Dartmoor Explorations
www.dartmoorexplorations.co.uk

Prehistoric Dartmoor
www.dartmoorwalks.org.uk

Dartmoor Trust
www.dartmoortrust.org

Dartefacts
www.dartefacts.co.uk

The Megalithic Portal
www.megalithic.co.uk

The Stone Rows of Great Britain
www.stonerows.wordpress.com

INDEX

Vixen Tor

RIGHTS AND RESPONSIBILITIES

Dartmoor is one of the few places in England where you can roam freely over much of it, without having to stick to public footpaths and rights of way. It has around 50,000 hectares of open access land, as designated under the Countryside Rights of Way Act 2000 (or CROW). These areas are marked by a light brown edge on the OS Explorer map. In addition, the Dartmoor Commons Act (1985) provides a right of access on foot and horseback to common land. The commons are areas of open unenclosed moorland that are privately owned, but on which some locals have rights to graze their livestock.

It goes without saying, but we all have a responsibility to care for places like Dartmoor.

ALWAYS FOLLOW THESE GENERAL RULES

- Drive considerately; do not block roads or gateways
- Take your litter home
- Close gates behind you
- Do not feed the ponies
- Keep your dog on a lead during ground-nesting bird season 1st March-31st July, and take dog waste home
- Do not have BBQs or campfires in open countryside.

SAFETY

The weather can change quickly on Dartmoor, so always take layers to keep you warm, a first aid kit and supplies of food and water. Check the forecast before you go. The ground can be boggy, even in dry weather, so waterproof footwear is advised. Take a paper map and don't rely on your phone.

There are three Military Training Areas on Dartmoor: Merrivale, Okehampton and Willsworthy. Check live firing times on the Government website before setting off and pay attention to any warning signs.

Be wary of cattle. They are most dangerous when there are calves around. In the last few years, there have been several attacks by cattle on walkers. It is always safest to go around them, not through the herd, and give them plenty of space. Change your route if you can't go around them. If you have a dog with you, keep it on a short lead and give the cattle a wide berth. If an animal does become aggressive, let your dog off the lead as the cattle are more likely to go for the dog than you.

Copyright
First edition published in the United Kingdom in 2025 by Wild Things Publishing Ltd. ISBN 9781910636534.

Text & photos:
Sophie Pierce & Alex Murdin

Illustrations:
Alex Murdin

Design and layout:
Ifan Bates, Tania Pascoe

Author acknowledgements:

Thank you to the family of Eric Hemery for allowing us to quote from his masterwork *High Dartmoor*. We are also grateful to his granddaughter Emma Cunis for generously sharing her knowledge of Dartmoor, as did Alan Endacott, Paul Rendell, Max Piper and many others. Rachel Dawson and Matt Newbury provided invaluable help with the text. Any mistakes are, of course, our own. Thank you to Jamie Dunbar and Tony Clark from the Dartmoor Trust for their help sourcing historic photographs and to Edwin Janes who scanned several of the old engravings. Thanks to Lesley and Paul Murdin for their support and encouragement and to Lucian and Felix for their early road testing of the tors.

Photo credits:

All photos by Alex Murdin and Sophie Pierce except page 6, Emma Stoner. Page 12: Bowerman's Nose by William Widgery (1870) courtesy of Royal Albert Memorial Museum, available through Creative Commons Public Domain Dedication; Vixen Tor by F J Widgery (1896) courtesy of Royal Albert Memorial Museum, available through Creative Commons Public Domain Dedication.

Published by:
Wild Things Publishing Ltd
Bath, BA2 7WG,
United Kingdom
hello@wildthingspublishing.com